Discovering the
JOHN MUIR TRAIL

"Through pen and lens, Corso provides the 'how to' and large doses of motivation. Caution! This trail guide may lead to much hiking and wilderness adventure."
        —**Charles Baker - member of the ALDHA-West Board of Directors**

"Corso captures the essence of the trail experience by weaving his own stories in with big, beautiful photos, photography tips, flower guides, and the personal experiences of other outdoor adventurers, leaving you with an emotional connection not only to the JMT, but with wilderness in general and its adventurers."
        —**Felicia "Princess of Darkness" Hermosillo - long distance hiker,
        co-host of "The Trail Show" podcast**

THEN IT SEEMED TO ME THE SIERRA SHOULD BE CALLED NOT THE NEVADA, OR SNOWY RANGE, BUT THE RANGE OF LIGHT. AND AFTER TEN YEARS SPENT IN THE HEART OF IT, REJOICING AND WONDERING, BATHING IN ITS GLORIOUS FLOODS OF LIGHT, SEEING THE SUNBURSTS OF MORNING AMONG THE ICY PEAKS, THE NOONDAY RADIANCE ON THE TREES AND ROCKS AND SNOW, THE FLUSH OF THE ALPENGLOW, AND A THOUSAND DASHING WATERFALLS WITH THEIR MARVELOUS ABUNDANCE OF IRISED SPRAY, IT STILL SEEMS TO ME ABOVE ALL OTHERS THE RANGE OF LIGHT, THE MOST DIVINELY BEAUTIFUL OF ALL THE MOUNTAIN-CHAINS I HAVE EVER SEEN.

—John Muir

Discovering the
JOHN MUIR TRAIL

An Inspirational Guide to America's Most Beautiful Hike

DAMON CORSO

FALCON®

Guilford, Connecticut

An imprint of The Rowman & Littlefield Publishing Group, Inc.
4501 Forbes Blvd., Suite 200
Lanham, MD 20706
www.rowman.com

Falcon and FalconGuides are registered trademarks and Make Adventure Your Story is a trademark of The Rowman & Littlefield Publishing Group, Inc.

Distributed by NATIONAL BOOK NETWORK

British Library Cataloguing-in-Publication Information Available

Library of Congress Cataloging-in-Publication Data Available
ISBN 978-1-4930-3124-5 (paperback
ISBN 978-1-4930-3125-2 (e-book)

∞™ The paper used in this publication meets the minimum requirements of American National Standard for Information Sciences—Permanence of Paper for Printed Library Materials, ANSI/NISO Z39.48-1992.

Printed in the United States of America

The author and Globe Pequot Press assume no liability for accidents happening to, or injuries sustained by, readers who engage in the activities described in this book.

Contents

SOCIETY SPEAKS AND ALL MEN LISTEN, MOUNTAINS SPEAK AND WISE MEN LISTEN.

—John Muir

Introduction

THE COMBINATION OF SLEET AND HAIL MADE NAVIGATING car-size blocks of granite quite dangerous, and the clouds were thick like New England clam chowder. How apropos. As the climbing leveled out, I finally took a moment to look forward and see the faint red and yellow blobs, signifying Smilin' Mike and El Paso were less than 30 feet ahead. I then took a peek behind me to see if our other friends were still in tow. I counted four more blobs and knew we were still together. A feeling had been welling up inside of me for the last mile of the steep climb. I knew it was all coming to an end, and even though I couldn't see the physical ending, I could feel it emotionally. Everyone's silence and the morose weather signified the end of an important chapter for all of us. Our paces quickened in rhythm, simultaneously being pulled toward the same spot in the middle of the wilderness. I heard the cheers of joy when Mike and El Paso reached the old wooden sign, the one that read "Mt. Katahdin," signifying the end of our thru-hike on the Appalachian Trail. Dropping to my knees next to the sign and smiling to the heavens as the sleet continued to remind me that Mother Nature ruled all, I knew I had reached the end of this journey. But there were many more to be had.

The hunger for more only intensified that stormy October afternoon in Maine; it's when I vowed to hike another long-distance trail at some point in my lifetime. Deep down in my soul, I knew it was going to be the John Muir Trail (JMT); the awe-inspiring feeling those mountains evoke is impossible to ignore as I witnessed firsthand during two individual week-long backpacking trips with my uncle into the Sierra backcountry as a teen. But as life tends to do, that idea had to sit on the back burner for many years as I focused on a photography career in the rock-climbing world and courting my beautiful wife with a proposal in the High Sierra and a wedding deep in the wild Na Pali coastline of Kauai. The Sierra backcountry has become my playground since I arrived in California in 2003. Hiking, backpacking, snowshoeing, snowboarding, rock climbing, and mountaineering have kept me craving the lakes, glaciers, peaks, and passes that comprise the jagged Sierra crest line. Always saddened to leave and constantly planning the next trip back, the Sierra Nevada truly is my home. The JMT has stood like a giant sequoia tree in the back of my mind, a dream never to be cut down. It wasn't until 2017 that I was able to hike the entire trail, experiencing new adventures and learning so much more about the mountains I have called home for so long.

Horsetail Firefall off of El Capitan,
Yosemite Valley

Entering nature is akin to entering the same church as the most prolific writers, artists, explorers, and athletes. Inspiration is untapped and clarity is heightened when one first lays eyes on a neon-blue alpine lake or when scrambling along a serrated granite ridgeline so far up that the eagles come to play in the thermals beside you. It is no wonder the Sierra Nevada chain has such a strong grasp on the influential players in the history of not only California but the rest of the country. Once you leave the city noise and start hiking away from the busy trailhead campgrounds, the world seems to slow down, worries wash away, and your breathing becomes more efficient as the colors and views become almost unnatural. Hiking along the JMT offers up the cream of the crop in California's hiking views. From the bottom of Yosemite Valley to the summit of Mt. Whitney, you are guaranteed to feel the same awe John Muir felt when he first set foot in the Sierra Nevada.

This book will be your jumping-off point to what some call the best hike in the world. Clocking in at 216 miles of total hiking (including the hike down from the summit of Mt. Whitney at trail's end), with eight major passes and over 47,000 feet of elevation gain (more than climbing Mt. Everest from sea level to summit), the JMT is an enormous physical and mental undertaking. The trail takes you through Yosemite Valley, Sequoia and Kings Canyon National Parks, Devils Postpile National Monument, the Ansel Adams and John Muir Wilderness Areas, and the Inyo and Sierra National Forests, all on your way to the summit of Mt. Whitney, the highest point in the contiguous United States. Along with the history of the trail and the mountains it weaves through, this book contains compelling stories from the author's experiences, along with information about the geology, flora, fauna, weather, hazards, and hiking details. All the information you need for a thru-hike or section hikes of the JMT can be found in each chapter, as well as National Geographic maps, mileage markers, elevation profiles, resupply information, photo tips, and backcountry excerpts. Top all this off with stunning photographs and artwork from the "Range of Light"—Ansel Adams's historical black-and-white images, Galen Rowell's rich colors, Scott Lange and Nick Foster's epic astrophotography, Peter Essick's new-era black-and-white techniques, Renan Ozturk's bright abstract paintings, and the author's documented hike of the trail.

For those adventurers not planning on hiking along the JMT, this book will get you inspired and into the wilderness. Whether it is to hike a section of the JMT, fish at one of the thousands of alpine lakes, observe wildlife, or climb a mountaineering route atop a nearby peak, you can find it all here. Like historian Francis Farquhar said, "Recreation in the Sierra is truly a re-creation of body and spirit." The High Sierra and the JMT may not be accessible for you at the moment. If this is the case, I recommend warming up near the fireplace with some tea and biscuits in the comfort of your own

Yosemite Valley
from tunnel view

home. Along with John Muir, my friends and I will navigate you on an adventure of a lifetime, and maybe you will discover the long-lost home you never knew you had.

THE MOUNTAINS ARE CALLING AND I MUST GO.

—John Muir

Moon over Half Dome - Reproduced with permission from The Ansel Adams Publishing Rights Trust. All rights reserved.

After a dry summer, Bridalveil Falls flows once
again following a major storm in Yosemite Valley.

The Sierra Nevada and the John Muir Trail

The human history of the Sierra Nevada has run through many generations and includes the Native American tribes dispersed across the range, John Muir and Joseph LeConte's golden age of exploration, and the current age of adventure tourism. This is just a brief outline of the major events affecting the range and the JMT. For unparalleled historical information, I suggest reading Francis Farquhar's book *History of the Sierra Nevada.*

Five major Native American tribes inhabited the Sierra Nevada many thousands of years prior to the white man's arrival. On the western side were three major tribes: the Yokut of the San Joaquin Valley to the Fresno River; the Miwok of the Fresno River to the American River; and just north of them was the Maidu tribe. On the eastern flank of the Sierra, there were two main tribes: the Paiute, who occupied the area surrounding Mono Lake and ventured into the High Sierra, and the Washoe tribe, who inhabited the area around Lake Tahoe and the Walker and Carson Rivers. The tribes were fairly peaceful with each other and made trade routes over the Sierra Crest, most notably the route up "the Old Mono Trail" through "Bloody Canyon," now known as Tioga Pass. The tribes frequently moved into the mountains during the summer months to seek cooler weather.

The first documented white men to cross the mighty Sierra were Jedediah Strong Smith and his group of "mountain men," who in 1826 were in search of new beaver-trapping country. On their journey from Colorado, they passed through southern California and into the Central Valley, where they met many native tribes and found fine spots to trap. On their return trip, they attempted to cross the great Sierra range unsuccessfully due to the immense amount of snow that season. The men returned to the valley and waited until May 20, 1827, when they began their second attempt from the north bank of the Stanislaus River. Within a week they made it to the crest at what is now Ebbetts Pass and continued down the eastern slope of the range.

The most important landmark in the Sierra is unquestionably Yosemite Valley and its unmistakable granite monuments. The history of the valley started with the native Ahwahnechee tribe, maliciously moved into the hands of the white man,

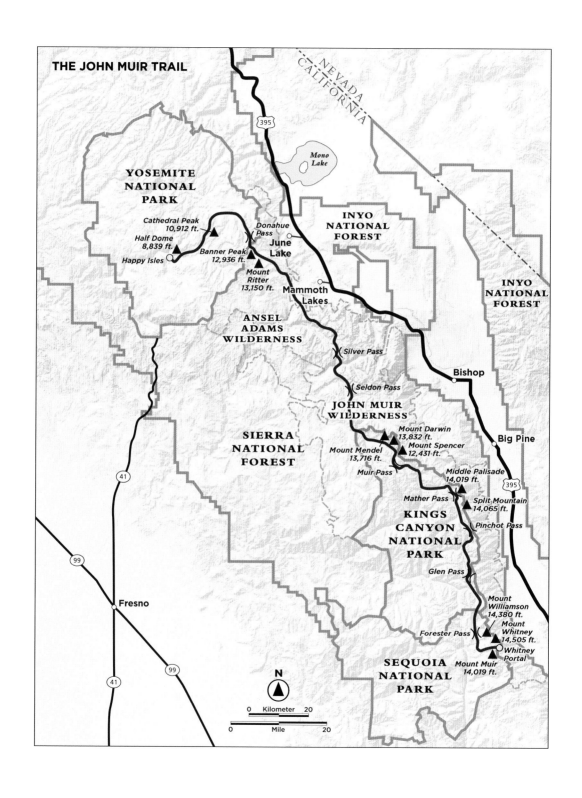

THE JOHN MUIR TRAIL

NEVADA
CALIFORNIA

395

Mono Lake

YOSEMITE
NATIONAL
PARK

INYO
NATIONAL
FOREST

Cathedral Peak
10,912 ft.
Half Dome
8,839 ft.
Happy Isles

Donahue
Pass
June
Lake

Banner Peak
12,936 ft.

Mount
Ritter
13,150 ft.

Mammoth
Lakes

INYO
NATIONAL
FOREST

ANSEL
ADAMS
WILDERNESS

Silver Pass

Seldon Pass

Bishop

JOHN MUIR
WILDERNESS

SIERRA
NATIONAL
FOREST

Mount Darwin
13,832 ft.

Mount Spencer
12,431 ft.

Mount Mendel
13,716 ft.

Big Pine

Muir Pass

Middle Palisade
14,019 ft.

Mather Pass

Split Mountain
14,065 ft.

KINGS
CANYON
NATIONAL
PARK

Pinchot Pass

395

Glen Pass

41

Mount
Williamson
14,380 ft.

Fresno

Mount
Whitney
14,505 ft.

Forester Pass

Whitney
Portal

99

SEQUOIA
NATIONAL
PARK

Mount Muir
14,019 ft.

41

99

N

0   Kilometer   20

0   Mile   20

John Muir
hand drawn
portrait
JEREMY COLLINS

and finally commenced with full protection when Abraham Lincoln enacted the Yosemite Grant.

The name "Yosemite" comes from Lafayette Houghton Bunnell, an American physician, author, and explorer. The Yo-sem-i-te tribe inhabited the Valley at the time the white men discovered it. The tribe was a mixture of Native Americans spanning from the Tuolumne River to the Kings River. Bunnell is well known for his involvement with the Mariposa Battalion, the first non-Indians to enter Yosemite Valley.

"During the winter of 1849–50, while ascending the old Bear Valley trail from Ridley's ferry, on the Merced River, my attention was attracted to the stupendous rocky peaks of the Sierra Nevadas. In the distance an immense cliff loomed, apparently to the summit of the mountains. Although familiar with nature in her wildest moods, I looked upon this awe-inspiring column with wonder and admiration."

Theodore Roosevelt and John Muir
on Glacier Point 1903, Yosemite
Valley UNKNOWN

The battalion's mission was to find the Ahwahnechee tribe (relatives of the Miwok and Paiute), led by Chief Tenaya, who had recently raided American settlements. The group invaded and set fire to the village, capturing their leader and forcing the tribe's migration to reservations in the Central Valley.

Another influential player in Yosemite history is Canadian Galen Clark. Clark moved to California during the gold rush but contracted tuberculosis in 1853 at the age of 39 and was given six months to live. In 1856 he decided to move to Wawona, saying, "I went to the mountains to take my chances of dying or growing better, which I thought were about even." After some years exploring the Mariposa Groves, Galen lobbied California senator John Conness for protection of Yosemite Valley. The senator immediately complied and introduced a bill to the senate in 1864 leading President Abraham Lincoln to sign the Yosemite Grant on June 30 of that year, giving control of the land to the state of California. "The premises shall be held for public use, resort, and recreation . . . shall be inalienable for all time." Galen was appointed "Guardian of the Yosemite Valley and the Big Tree Grove," where he lived a full life and died at the ripe old age of 95.

Then came John Muir, born in Dunbar, Scotland, in 1838, who first set foot in the valley of Yosemite State Park in 1868 for a short visit. Muir was so enamored with the park that he decided to return the following summer to live and work as a shepherd's ranch hand, prompting his book *My First Summer in the Sierra*, and showing him the threat these "hooved locusts" imposed on the future of the valley. Muir spent the next years of his life writing thought-provoking articles, studying nature, and forming the Sierra Club in 1892, all on his way to help preserve Yosemite forever. After taking President Theodore Roosevelt on a backcountry adventure through Yosemite in 1903, Muir was able to persuade him to sign a new bill that released the valley from state control and awarded it back to the federal government as a national park. This was known as the Yosemite Recession Act of 1906—from this point on, the land was federally protected and paved the way for the national park movement in America.

Josiah Whitney, a professor from Harvard University, was appointed chief of the California Geological Survey in 1860 and led a highly academic and experienced team in surveying the geology of the state. Whitney and his team were the first to determine there were two major chains in the Southern Sierra, the Great Western Divide and the main Sierra Crest, the latter of which rose upward of 14,000 feet. Over the next five years, Whitney and his team ascended many of the surrounding peaks, and several were named after members of the team. They were likely the first to cross the Kings/Kern Divide, linking the Great Western Divide and the Sierra Crest. One determined member of the team, geologist and mountaineer Clarence King, continued his mission to summit the largest of the peaks and succeeded in 1873, a month shy of the true first ascent. He named the peak after Josiah.

Explorer Theodore Solomons first envisioned a trail that walked along the backbone of the mighty Sierra Nevada chain. "The idea of a crest-parallel trail came to me one day while herding my uncle's cattle in an immense unfenced alfalfa field near Fresno. It was 1884 and I was 14." By 1892 Theodore Solomons spent the next few summers exploring the high country of Yosemite and the Sierra in much detail, attempting to find a route from Tuolumne to Kings Canyon.

WHEN I FIRST ENJOYED THIS SUPERB VIEW, ONE GLOWING APRIL DAY, FROM THE SUMMIT OF THE PACHECO PASS, THE CENTRAL VALLEY, BUT LITTLE TRAMPLES OF PLOWED AS YET, WAS ONE FURRED, RICH SHEET OF GOLDEN COMPOSITAE, AND THE LUMINOUS WALL OF THE MOUNTAINS SHONE IN ALL ITS GLORY. THEN IT SEEMED TO ME THE SIERRA SHOULD BE CALLED NOT THE NEVADA, OR SNOWY RANGE, BUT THE RANGE OF LIGHT.

—*John Muir*

Enlisting the help of Joseph "Little Joe" LeConte, a geology professor from the University of California, they explored and mapped a majority of the region. They repeatedly were stopped at the Goddard Divide, failing to find a safe route for the pack train down toward the Kings River.

Horseback riding was the first method of transportation to Yosemite Valley, other than coming by foot GEORGE FISKE

It wasn't until 1907 that a party with pack animals was able to cross over the Goddard Divide (now Muir Pass) and into what is now LeConte Canyon by a US Geologic Survey led by George R. Davis. With this new information, the following year LeConte enlisted James S. Hutchinson and Duncan McDuffie to travel the length of the High Sierra with pack animals from Yosemite to Kings Canyon in one continuous push, not exactly the same route that is currently the JMT, but very close.

On a Sierra Club outing in the summer of 1914, Meyer Lissner made the suggestion that the state should fund the construction of trails in the High Sierra in order for the mountains to be more accessible. Sadly, at the end of that year, their first president, John Muir, passed away. The following year when Joseph LeConte was president of the club, a trail name was decided upon in honor of their late president and environmental activist, and $10,000 was appropriated to the building of a trail that would follow the route Solomons and LeConte had spent years exploring. Similar funding occurred in 1917, 1925, 1927, and 1929 to continue efforts to link the whole trail. Construction of the official trail began mere months after Muir's death and was finished in 1938, one hundred years after Muir's birth.

GEOLOGY BY MICHAEL HASSON

The Sierra Nevada is roughly 400 miles long, 50 to 80 miles wide, and rises from just above sea level at the base of the western slope to over 14,500 feet at the top of Mt. Whitney. From a geological perspective, the Sierra Nevada is particularly remarkable because of its young age. The gray seas of granite—out of which were carved sweeping valleys and craggy peaks and ridges that are so characteristic of the High Sierra—did not begin to be uplifted until around 5 million years ago. This likely sounds incomprehensibly distant, but compared to the Rocky Mountains a thousand miles east, which began to form 80 million years ago, the Sierra Nevada has just come into existence. At this point it's necessary to clarify that these dates only account for the enormous swathes of relatively similar rock but not the valleys that were carved out much more recently. Between 1 million years ago and just 16,000 years ago, massive glaciers formed and carved entire valleys out of these granitic slabs. On a timeline beginning with the formation of the earth, 4.6 billion years in the past, some of the most noticeable features protected by the different wilderness areas and national parks along the John Muir Trail have just come into being.

So why is the Sierra Nevada so young? What caused these mountains to spring into existence in the first place? To understand the current topography, one must first understand how the rock that the different features are carved into was formed in the first place, and understanding this broader geologic history of the Sierra requires us to step back to a point in time when the range, as it exists today, was completely unrecognizable.

One of the first clues to understanding the evolution of the Sierra Nevada is found in its geographic location relative to tectonic plate boundaries. For centuries, geologists had a lot of trouble coming up with ideas that might provide a plausible explanation for how and why continents seemed to be "mobile" over very long timescales. After decades of refinement and searching for evidence, a widely accepted theory to explain this phenomenon was developed. The theory states that the outer portion of the earth that encompasses the crust (Earth's outermost layer) and upper portions of the mantle (Earth's second-outermost layer) consists of seven large "plates" and many, many smaller ones. These plates are generally rigid but move with respect to one another. It is the interaction of these jostling plates at their margins that is responsible for much geologic activity, including the formation of major mountain ranges such as the Sierra Nevada.

When two plates that are composed of rock of different densities come together, the plate with the more dense rock will typically subduct, or slide underneath, the plate composed of less-dense rock, forming what geologists refer to as a subduction zone. In areas such as this, the more dense, typically oceanic plate, along with significant amounts of water and other "volatiles" (substances whose presence can lead to instability within molten rock deep underground) will essentially get pushed underneath the less dense plate. The volatiles present in the subducting plate often lead to very active volcanism around subduction zones.

The first step in the process of building the Sierra was a collision between the Farallon Plate and the North American Plate. As the most dense plate, the Pacific Plate slid underneath the North American Plate, taking with it large amounts of water and other chemical compounds that can cause molten rock to become unstable when subjected to a tremendous increase in temperature and pressure caused by the mass of the North American Plate pushing downward. This change in conditions led huge sections of rock to melt and work their way toward the surface.

So what does that mean for the Sierra Nevada? Essentially, during the Mesozoic era (~250 million years ago to 66 million years ago), there was an area of great volcanic activity where the Sierra now stand. The molten rock (magma) that formed when the dense Pacific Plate slid underneath the less dense North American Plate repeatedly rose closer and closer to the surface until some of it was expelled in the form of volcanic eruptions. The rock that actually reached the surface, however, made up only a small portion of the total magma present, and much more rock solidified beneath the surface than above it.

These two scenarios—solidification above and beneath the surface—present two very different sets of conditions that led to very different rock types. Above the surface magma solidifies very quickly since the temperature is so low compared to the subsurface. Because of this, there is not enough time for crystals to grow, and it is

Conrad Anker climbing on the majestic and commiting Palisades Traverse VI 5.9
JIMMY CHIN

rare to be able to see them without a microscope. The most common rocks that form in this manner are basalts and andesites—both dark-colored, iron-and-magnesium-rich rocks that make up visible outcrops near the John Muir Trail at Devils Postpile near Mammoth and Little Devils Postpile near Glen Aulin, just north of Tuolumne Meadows. On the other hand, when magma solidifies underneath the surface, it cools much more slowly, allowing relatively large crystals to grow. The different types of gray granitic rocks that are so characteristic of the Sierra Nevada formed in this manner, and when one examines them, there are visible crystals of different minerals—primarily potassium and plagioclase feldspar (pink or white), quartz (usually clear or white), and biotite/hornblende (black).

In the case of the Sierra Nevada, the volcanoes visible at the surface were being fed by an enormous magma chamber called a batholith that sat roughly 3 to 10 miles beneath the volcanoes. While batholiths do not force their way to the earth's surface, they must "push" some of the material situated above them out of the way in order to form the bases of the volcanoes above them. For this reason, the rock that would form much of the Sierra Nevada is called "intrusive" rock, since it pushes its way through other preexisting metamorphic rock. This older rock is best visible as it forms the dark-red peaks of the Ritter Range—most notably, Mt. Ritter and Banner Peak, which sit across Garnet Lake from the JMT, between Island Pass and Red's Meadow. When intrusive rocks are interpreted to be formed by the same magma-producing event, they are often called intrusive suites, which geologists can identify by studying their mineral and textural compositions. One of the most noticeable is the Tuolumne Intrusive Suite, a type of granite that forms much of Tuolumne Meadows and Yosemite Valley. The different types of granitic rock present in the Sierra are also easily visible in Yosemite Valley when looking up at El Capitan—notice the enormous darker spots on the wall that are visible from the valley floor.

By the late Cretaceous period (70 million years ago), the volcanic rocks that had previously covered the granitic plutons had all but entirely eroded away, essentially leaving a relatively flat, exposed platform. At this point in time, the Sierra Nevada as we know it today was starting to become slightly more recognizable but was still essentially just a large mass of granitic rocks—nothing particularly breathtaking. Even so, the area was beginning to be defined by massive intrusive granitic rocks, just as it is today. Progress!

In the next period of the development of the Sierra, plate tectonics again became the driving factor. Around 5 million years ago (during the late Miocene period), the crust began to be stretched out from east to west. In the region around the nascent mountains, the surface responded by forming faults where different sections of the crust broke, pushing the block on one side of the fault upward and the other block downward. This occurred primarily on the eastern side of the Sierra Nevada, where Owens Valley, which US-395 runs through, now sits. When Owens Valley sank down, the other side of the fault that the early Sierra sat on moved upward. Because of the way that the extension occurred, the western side of the range did not undergo the same kind of faulting as the eastern portion, accounting for the less abrupt edge of the range on the western side than on the eastern side.

Finally, we come to the most recent major process that shaped the Sierra into the dynamic, rugged range that we experience today. The Pleistocene epoch (between ~2.5 million and ~11,700 years ago) was a time of extensive global glaciation. As glaciers formed and slowly flowed downhill, they carved the once-flat base of the Sierra into the stunning valleys and peaks that are so essential to the Sierra today. One of the primary indicators that much of the Sierran topography was formed through glacial processes is the shape of the valleys. While rivers that cut valleys into solid bodies of rock almost always form a V-shaped valley, glaciers almost always form U-shaped valleys like Yosemite Valley. So, unbelievable as it may seem, the features that draw many visitors to recreate in the Sierra may be just over 10,000 years old—barely there in terms of the 4.6-billion-year history of the world.

NATURAL HISTORY

While traveling from Yosemite to Mt. Whitney, you will cross through four diverse biotic life zones with ever-changing plants and animals occupying the landscape. The western and eastern slopes have slightly different characteristics due to the difference in topographical relief as well as the southern and northern reaches of the range. The trees are the most constant of plant life along the enchainment of the Sierra, withstanding storm after storm in every season over the course of their lives, while the flowers, herbs, and grasses are determined by the specific landscape and season they are found in.

The first life zone you enter is the **lower montane belt,** from 3,500 to 6,000 feet, dominated by Jeffrey, sugar, and ponderosa pines and Douglas fir. Yosemite Valley and the first miles of the JMT are in this zone and receive a fair amount of precipitation during the wet seasons. They can hold snow for many months, which lays the groundwork for a diverse population of trees and plants. This zone is also where you will find a majority of the legendary giant sequoia groves.

The next life zone you enter is the **upper montane belt,** which ranges from 5,500 to 8,000 feet. You will quickly enter this zone as you hike beyond the Half Dome trail junction out of Yosemite and move on toward Sunrise High Sierra Camp. The forests are dominated by lodgepole, Jeffrey, and white pines along with beautiful western junipers and red firs. This zone is where you will encounter many meadows with their lush grass and sedge carpets lined with wildflowers during their bloom. The summers in this zone accumulate more moisture than the previously mentioned zones and collect snow in the winter that can last through June.

Staying just below tree line, you will enter the **subalpine belt,** where the forests are determined by the harsh environments they survive in. The elevation ranges from 8,000 to 12,000 feet, and the growing season is a mere 6 to 9 weeks long. Freezing temperatures can occur at any time, and snow piles upward of 15 feet in heavy winters. Along with high winds, the soils here are a lot thinner and lack a variety of nutrients, causing many trees to form with the gnarled and stunted krummholz shape. The most common trees that grow in this zone are the mountain hemlock, western white pine, foxtail pine, and whitebark pine. This zone is very fragile and is susceptible to drastic environmental changes.

The final and upper zone of life in the Sierra Nevada is the **alpine belt,** typically found at 12,000 feet and higher above tree line. In this range the growing season is exceptionally short and harsh where various features of granite outcrops dominate the terrain. The flowers bloom and produce seeds at a hurried rate and tend to grow very small in large mats mere centimeters off the ground. Typically the leaves are red or white for sun radiation protection and form a waxy or hairy coating to protect them from the harsh environment.

Below is a chart of the most common conifer trees you will find in the different life zones of the Sierra Nevada, along with illustrations of their needles and cones from *The Laws Field Guide to the Sierra Nevada.*

FAUNA

On each trip to the John Muir Trail you will discover a variety of creatures sharing the land in perfect harmony, harvesting foods, tending to their newborns, making new homes, and generally enjoying the abundant land that is the Sierra Nevada. Depending on what life zone you are in, the wildlife will range from the tiny pavement ant to the mighty California black bear. Much of the wildlife, like the endangered bighorn sheep, keeps itself well hidden from human eyes. But there are certain animals that

NAME	ELEVATION	CONE SIZE
Douglas fir	3,000–7,000 ft.	2–3 in.
Sugar pine	3,000–7,000 ft.	10–18 in.
White fir	3,000–8,000 ft.	3–5 in.
Red fir/silver fir	5,000–9,000 ft.	6–8 in.

NAME	ELEVATION	CONE SIZE
Lodgepole pine	7,000–11,000 ft.	2½ –3½ in.
Mountain hemlock	9,000–10,500 ft.	2–3 in.
Foxtail pine	9,000–11,500 ft.	2½–4½ in.
Whitebark pine	9,500–12,000 ft.	1½–3 in.

have become accustomed to humans, and you will repeatedly see them as you travel through similar life zones. This mainly includes small mammals, mule deer, and a wide selection of birds. There are hundreds of species sharing the land, ranging from insects, spiders, moths, butterflies, fish, reptiles, amphibians, and rare birds of prey, all of which can unfortunately not fit into these pages. Some of the more common animals will be featured in photos throughout the book, and if you find yourself interested in this area of research, be sure to purchase a proper guide like *Sierra Nevada Natural History.*

FLORA

With over a thousand species of flowers, herbs and shrubs, and trees, the Sierra Nevada is California's number-one location to observe the colorful and lively display when the region comes to life after being buried deep in snow for much of the year. Peak bloom of these magical wildflowers is typically in mid- to late June from 7,000 feet and up in elevation. The northern and southern Sierra have different variations since each species is very specific to where and when it can grow. There are a few species or a slight variation you will see continually as you traverse the entire length of the trail, like the Sierra daisy. But there are certain flowers that only grow at specific elevations, like the sky pilot, only able to grow at 13,000 feet, or the wide variety of lilies that can only be seen near water sources. As you spend more time in the Sierra, you will become trained to know what species to expect in certain environments, finding commonalities in all the marshy meadows, alpine talus, and dry hillsides you will encounter. Many examples of plants, identified by naturalist David Lukas, are shown in each section of this book in hopes that you can spot some of the more beautiful and common ones along your hike.

OUTDOOR ETHICS

You will travel through some of the most unspoiled land the country has to offer, and it is up to all of us to keep that land pristine and safe for the following generations. The amount of people visiting the Sierra Nevada increases every year. "Leave No Trace" ethics are paramount as the landscape is very fragile and in some cases can never recover from damage due to the harsh conditions, especially in the subalpine and alpine zones. A simple format to follow is the backcountry Leave No Trace principles outlined below:

- **Plan ahead and prepare.** Check current trail conditions, weather, and regulations. Prepare your meals prior to your trip and cook on stoves instead of an open fire. Travel in small groups when possible.

- **Travel and camp on durable surfaces.** Stay on the main trail—don't cut switch-backs. If you must travel off-trail, try to stay on durable surfaces and spread your group out to disperse any damage. Avoid camping on living vegetation.
- **Dispose of waste properly.** If you pack it in, pack it out. Organic waste can take months or years to decompose and can disrupt animal-foraging habits. Do not burn trash, and pick up any trash you do find on the trail. Bathe and clean dishes at least 100 feet from water sources or campsites, and toss the remains in a wide arc. Dig a hole for human waste 6 inches deep and pack out your TP.
- **Leave what you find.** Take only pictures, leave only footprints, minimizing your impact so it is as if you were never there. Avoid introducing or transporting non-native species.
- **Minimize campfire impacts.** Fire restrictions apply in all areas and can change—be sure to check with the local wilderness center for current rules. If you have a legal fire, use an existing fire ring only, collecting wood on the ground. Make sure to put your fire out completely and spread the cool ashes over a large area.
- **Respect wildlife.** Never feed wildlife, and always store your food properly. The national parks require use of an approved bear canister in certain areas. If you are in an area that allows dogs, keep your dog on a leash or within voice com-mand distance.
- **Be considerate of other visitors.** Be courteous to other hikers and yield to other users and pack stock on the trail. When possible, give others space and privacy at camp, and avoid making loud noises.

There are also a number of rules to follow when choosing a campsite in the Sierra backcountry. It is standard practice to make your first night's camp at least 4 miles from the trailhead on which you entered. There are many lakes that have no-camping zones at their outlets, and there are restoration sites where overuse has occurred and camping has been prohibited—make sure to read all signs. The national parks, national forests, and wilderness areas each have varying regulations printed for you when you receive your permit. More area-specific information can be found at nps .gov and sierrawild.gov.

WEATHER

Although many hazards exist when extreme weather strikes, generally the Sierra Nevada climate is mild for an alpine range, sitting close enough to the Pacific Ocean and Central Valley to be affected by the storms from the North and West. As storms get trapped or pass through the mountains, the height and shape of the range influ-ences the complexion of the storm before it moves across the western United States. Summer months, between late June and late August, are the most popular time to

Dropping into "Squeeze Play" on
the Middle Fork of the Kings River
DARIN MCQUOID

visit the Sierra and the JMT. The high passes become free of snow, temperatures range from the mid-70s to low 40s Fahrenheit, and afternoon showers cool the day down on occasion.

When September rolls around, precipitation will increase as the average temperatures start to drop, making way for the first snowfall of the season in late October or early November. December marks the official start to winter in the Sierra. During a good season an average of 400 to 550 inches of snow will fall in the high mountains, giving skiers and snowboarders some of the best powder on the West Coast. Temperatures in the dead of winter can drop as low as below zero in the evening at higher altitudes, especially when wind is involved. As the storms become less and less frequent in March and April, the temperatures begin to rise and the snow starts melting, ushering in all the new life spring has to offer. Rivers swell up in May and June as the snowmelt accelerates, and flooding can occur during heavy years. But this leaves the trails covered in the bright colors of new wildflowers.

HAZARDS

As beautiful and enjoyable as a day hike or extended backpacking excursion in the Sierra can be, it is equally dangerous if you are not properly prepared or informed on the conditions and hazards ahead. Always leave your itinerary with someone at home, and some people choose to bring an emergency beacon or a satellite phone for backup. A membership in the American Alpine Club includes rescue insurance and can help save your life and bank account if one ever occurs. Summertime is the most popular season to visit the Sierra, but hazards still exist, including lightning, fire, rockfall, and injury. Early spring is an amazing time to experience the Sierra's colorful bloom of wildflowers and snowcapped peaks, but this is when river crossings are a major hazard and avalanches can still strike. Late fall and winter pose heavier threats, with unpredictable snowstorms lasting for days, while temps can drop below zero degrees very quickly.

LIGHTNING

Lightning is one of the most common hazards you will face in the High Sierra. Here are signs to watch for and how to protect yourself from oncoming storms:

- Watch for building cumulus clouds in the afternoon, which may signal a storm.
- Get off any high mountain passes and take cover in lower elevations.
- Situate yourself in a cluster of small trees devoid of exposed roots and away from water, and crouch down.
- A tent is a safe place to stay—situate yourself on top of your sleeping pad or pack, keeping all metal objects outside the tent if possible.

- A storm is passing when the time between lightning strike and thunder extends each time.
- More information can be found at www.lightningsafety.noaa.gov.

FOREST FIRES

The Sierra has been susceptible to forest fires over the years. With major droughts and excessive heat, a single spark can ignite an entire area. Here are some tips to survive a wildfire in the wilderness:

- Retreat to the lowest area possible, as fires climb hills very quickly if there is wind.
- If you are in a highly flammable area, get out (dry grasses, dead trees . . . etc).
- Retreat to an already-burned area, which poses little threat of being burned again.
- Look for water—if you can find a lake or stream stay in the water until the fire threat passes.
- You can read more about fire prevention at www.smokeybear.com.

ROCKFALL

Rockfalls can occur anytime of the year but tend to happen in the winter and early spring after major rainfall, snowmelt, and subfreezing temperatures combine. The granite is also susceptible to exfoliation, vegetation growing in cracks, and earth-quakes. This natural and unpredictable occurrence is most likely to happen on steep cliffs and talus slopes, so be cautious when near these features. If you find yourself near a rockfall, here are some tips to remember:

- Quickly move away from the area and find a large rock to shelter behind.
- Once the hazard has stopped, quickly leave the area.
- When possible, report the incident to a local ranger or the forest visitor center for future assessment of rockfall hazards.

INJURY

Personal injury can end a trip quickly. It is good to know about some common injuries and how to treat them in the backcountry to ensure a safe return home.

- **Sprained ankle:** Take time to rest while soaking the injured area in a cold stream, lake, or even a wet bandanna. When ready to move, wrap the ankle with tape or elastic bandage, making wraps around the ankle and then under the arch of the foot.
- **Broken bone:** If there is an open wound, treat this first by washing and covering it—do not apply pressure to the area. If necessary, make a tourniquet to avoid

major blood loss. Make a splint by wrapping a hiking pole, branch, or a hard piece of plastic around the injured area. Make a plan to exit the wilderness or call for a rescue if needed.

- **Hypothermia:** Get into warm, dry clothes and stay in the tent and sleeping bag. Stay awake, eat sweet snacks, and drink warm liquids. In extreme cases use skin-to-skin contact to exchange body heat.
- **Altitude sickness:** Common signs of early-onset altitude sickness are nausea, fatigue, headache, lethargy, and loss of appetite, which can be cured by descending to the last altitude you felt good at in order to acclimatize before continuing on. The later and most dangerous stages of altitude sickness show a lack of balance, shortness of breath, and a wet cough. When these symptoms occur, immediately descend to a lower elevation and seek medical help.

RIVER CROSSING

Man-made bridges exist across a number of the biggest crossings, like the Merced River in Yosemite and the Woods Creek suspension bridge in Kings Canyon. You may also find logs or rocks to cross some of the smaller creeks, but it is inevitable that you will have to ford a creek with no bridge. In early spring this is a major hazard due to melting snow hitting its maximum rate as temperatures stop dropping below freezing. Some tips to remember when crossing are:

- Cross in the morning when water levels are at their lowest.
- Use sturdy shoes or sandals to help keep traction.
- Unclip your pack in case you slip, to avoid being weighted down and drowning.
- Investigate the stream for slower portions where the depth is also shallow.
- Face upstream and use hiking poles or a sturdy stick to keep your balance.
- Walk slowly and slightly backwards with the current with each step.
- Link arms with a partner and traverse the hazard together if need be.
- If you slip, ditch your pack, get on your back, and point your feet downstream to evaluate the best exit.

AVALANCHES

Spring poses the greatest avalanche threat to hikers in the high country. With snow lasting late into the season on the northern slopes, cliff bands, rocky features, and shallow snowpack on grassy slopes become the biggest threats. Weak overnight freezes and unseasonably warm days will cause the snow to thaw quickly in the morning and become saturated with water during the day, causing a slide. In the unlikely event that you get caught in an avalanche, here are some tips to remember:

- Move to the side quickly to get out of the main line of the avalanche.

Alex Honnold
solo on
Cathedral Peak
MIKEY SCHAEFFER

- Try to stay afloat on top of the snow and keep your head exposed.
- If buried by the snow, make an air pocket over your mouth and nose to prevent asphyxiation.
- More information on avalanche danger can be found at www.esavalanche.org.

SNOW

Late fall and early spring, when there are fewer crowds, are wonderful times to be in the Sierra. But remember there is still a chance for snowstorms to strike. If this happens and you do not have winter equipment with you, here are some tips to stay safe and warm:

- Stay next to the trail and find a protected area to set camp.
- Stay on your sleeping pad to help keep your body temperature from dropping.
- Prevent your tent from caving in by knocking the snow off every hour or so.
- If you run out of water, do not eat snow—melt it on a stove to keep your body temperature up.
- Once the storm stops, reevaluate the situation—you may have to turn back to avoid getting lost.

WILDERNESS PERMITS

Permits are required to backpack and camp in any area along the JMT at all times of the year. Day hikes do not require a permit except in the Mt. Whitney zone. Each area has its own regulations during peak season (May–Sept) and allows for self-issued permits off-season at visitor centers and permit stations. Each trailhead has a maximum daily quota to prevent overcrowding, so you should make your reservation (fee required) as early as possible through the agency in charge of where you will begin your hike. Permits are available for pickup the day prior to your hike and the morning of until 10 a.m., but check with the permitting office for specific hours.

To obtain a walk-up permit (no fee), arrive a day before your planned hike and apply for one at the permitting station where you want to start your hike. You can also wait to see if there are cancellations for same-day permits. Thru-hikes on the JMT only require one permit from Yosemite or Inyo National Forest, where a brand-new 21-day rolling lottery system was put into place in 2017.

YOSEMITE NATIONAL PARK

There is a small reservation fee per permit, per person in season. Each trail has a reserved quota (60 percent) and a walk-up quota (40 percent); the reservation office will accept applications as early as 24 weeks (168 days) before your intended entry date. You can fill out the permit application form found at www.nps.gov/yose/planyourvisit and fax it to (209) 372-0739. You can also call in a request at (209) 372-0740, although faxes take priority. Lastly, you can print a form and mail your request to:

Wilderness Permits
PO Box 545
Yosemite, CA, 95389

For further questions about Yosemite conditions or trailheads, contact the rangers at (209) 372-0826.

SEQUOIA AND KINGS CANYON NATIONAL PARKS

Permit reservations are available starting March 1 and up to two weeks prior to your trip for a fee. Seventy-five percent of permits for each trailhead are put aside for reservations and the remainder are saved for walk-up visitors. Your permit can be claimed the day prior to your hike after 1 p.m. or the day of before 9 a.m. Locate the form at www.nps.gov/seki, and email it to seki_wilderness_reservations@nps.gov or mail it to:

Sequoia & Kings Canyon National Parks
Wilderness Permit Reservations
47050 Generals Hwy. #60
Three Rivers, CA 93271

For further questions about SEKI NP trail conditions or permits, call (559) 565-3766.

SIERRA NATIONAL FOREST

Permit reservations can be made up to one year in advance but not later than 21 days prior to leaving for the trip for a small per-person fee (unless exiting from Mt. Whitney, which requires a larger fee per person). Sixty percent of permits are for reservations and 40 percent for walk-up permits (no fee). You can find the application form at www.fs.usda.gov/sierra, and it must be picked up at least 48 hours prior to your planned departure at the permitting office listed on your form. Mail the form to:

For trips originating north and west of the San Joaquin River:
Bass Lake Ranger District
Attn.: Wilderness Permits
57003 Road 225
North Fork, CA 93643
(559) 877-2218, ext. 0

For trips originating south and east of the San Joaquin River:
High Sierra Ranger District
Attn.: Wilderness Permits
PO Box 559
Prather, CA 93651
(559) 855-5355, ext. 0

INYO NATIONAL FOREST

Reservations are required from May 1 through November 1 for most areas within the national forest for a fee; walk-in permits are free. Sixty percent of the permits are saved for reservations and the other 40 percent are saved for walk-in permits. Specific permits for the Whitney zone apply—you can find more information at www.fs.usda.gov/inyo. To make a reservation, visit www.recreation.gov and search for "Inyo National Forest wilderness permits." You can make your reservation online.

For more information on trail conditions, call (760) 873-2483.

TRANSPORTATION

- East Side Sierra Shuttle services all trailheads. Contact Paul Fretheim: (760) 878-8047, paul@inyopro.com, eastsidesierrashuttle.com.

Cathedral Peak from
Upper Cathedral Lake

- Sierra Shuttle Service accommodates all trailheads: (760) 914-2746, SierraShuttleServices@outlook.com, sierrashuttleservice.com.
- Mammoth Shuttle System services all trailheads. Contact Rolf Knutson: (760) 914-2678, mammothshuttle@npgcable.com.
- Yosemite Valley Shuttle System offers free in-season transportation in the valley and Tuolumne. For schedules and maps, visit www.nps.gov/yose.
- Yosemite Area Rapid Transit (YARTS) is a bus system that services Mammoth Lakes and Tuolumne to Yosemite Valley, Fresno to Yosemite Valley, and Sonora to Yosemite Valley: (877) 989-2787, www.yarts.com.
- Eastern Sierra Transit Authority (ESTA) is a bus system that services major points from Reno to Lancaster, with express transits between Lone Pine and Mammoth Lakes: (800) 922-1930, www.estransit.com.

EQUIPMENT

A hike in the Sierra Nevada, whether it be an overnight trip, a long weekend, or a thru-hike, will require food and some essential equipment. Some people enjoy comforts in the backcountry and will therefore choose to carry more weight, while others seek a more minimalist experience and go "ultralight." The practice of going ultralight is becoming the norm for long-distance hikers in particular, where base pack weight (equipment with no food or water) is cut down to 10 to 15 pounds. With the proper research and patience, one can assemble any style of backpacking kit for an affordable price. Many companies produce a line of ultralight equipment alongside their standard gear. Pick the one that best suits your needs and budget.

Most hikers carry 2 pounds of food per day, so if you are doing an extended journey, you may need to mail ahead a food resupply. Resupply locations can be found in each section. Most can be accessed right along the trail with a minor detour, while others may require a long trip out of the mountains into town. If you are not good at planning a resupply, you can check out the service available at zerodayresupply.com. Zero Day Resupply is an online hiker-resupply service started by Chris Solinski, a.k.a. "Spartan," a triple-crown hiker, with the goal of making your resupply easy. This service allows thru-hikers to set up their resupplies as they move up the trail. With no need to plan meals and prepare boxes months in advance, you can enjoy flexibility and are able to adjust your diet to meet changing demands on the trail. "We are giving thru-hikers a better way to resupply by providing a smart and convenient method for getting what they need on trail."

Below is a list of items one may expect to carry on a multiday trip into the Sierra. Many items can be excluded depending on your personal comfort level and the season.

CAMPING GEAR

- Backpacking pack
- Tent with rain fly and ground cloth
- Cold-weather sleeping bag
- Sleeping pad
- Bear canister
- Camp stove and fuel
- Cooking pot
- Plate/bowl/cup and utensils
- Water purification (filter, UV, or tablets)
- Water container
- Headlamp and extra batteries
- Hiking poles

CLOTHING

- Rain gear (incl. jacket and pants)
- Down or fleece jacket/vest
- Warm hat
- Gloves or mittens
- Long underwear
- Sun-protective hat
- Long-sleeved shirt
- Short-sleeved shirt
- Long pants/convertible pants/shorts
- Extra socks
- Extra underwear
- Camp shoes/sandals
- Camp towel
- Micro-spikes (in high snowpack years)

OTHER NECESSITIES

- ID, credit card, cash
- Printed topo maps and compass
- Nylon cording
- Insect repellent
- Sunscreen/lip balm
- Sunglasses
- Small shovel/toilet paper
- Toothbrush/toothpaste
- This book

FIRST-AID KIT

- Moleskin
- ACE bandage
- Adhesive bandages
- Antibiotic ointment
- Painkillers
- Personal medications

EMERGENCY KIT

- Space blanket
- Whistle
- Signal mirror
- Lighter or waterproof matches
- Pocket knife/multitool
- Duct tape

EXTRA PERSONAL ITEMS

- Camera with batteries and memory cards or film
- Notepad/pencil/sketchbook
- Book
- Phone/music device
- GPS/emergency beacon

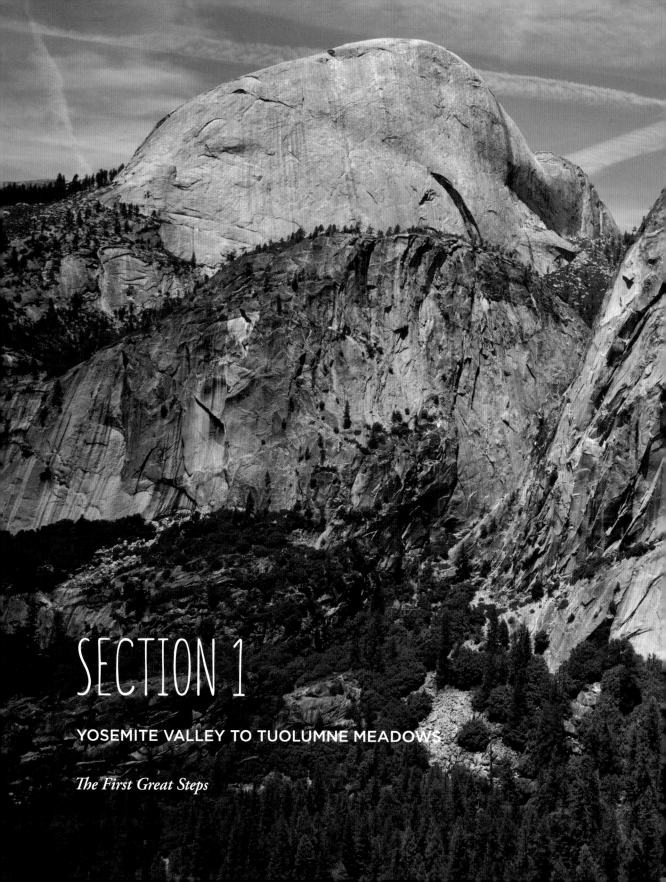

SECTION 1

YOSEMITE VALLEY TO TUOLUMNE MEADOWS

The First Great Steps

Half Dome, Liberty Cap, and
Nevada Falls

Half Dome and Yosemite Valley as seen from the Clouds Rest Trail

SECTION 1
YOSEMITE VALLEY TO TUOLUMNE MEADOWS

LOCATION: Yosemite National Park

LENGTH: 22.2 miles

ELEVATION GAIN/ LOSS (NORTH -> SOUTH): +8,225 ft./ −3,685 ft.

LOWEST POINT: Yosemite Valley Happy Isles Trailhead, 4,035 ft.

HIGHEST POINT: Cathedral Pass, 9,705 ft.

[YOSEMITE VALLEY IS A] GRAND PAGE OF MOUNTAIN MANUSCRIPT THAT I WOULD GLADLY GIVE MY LIFE TO BE ABLE TO READ.

—*John Muir*

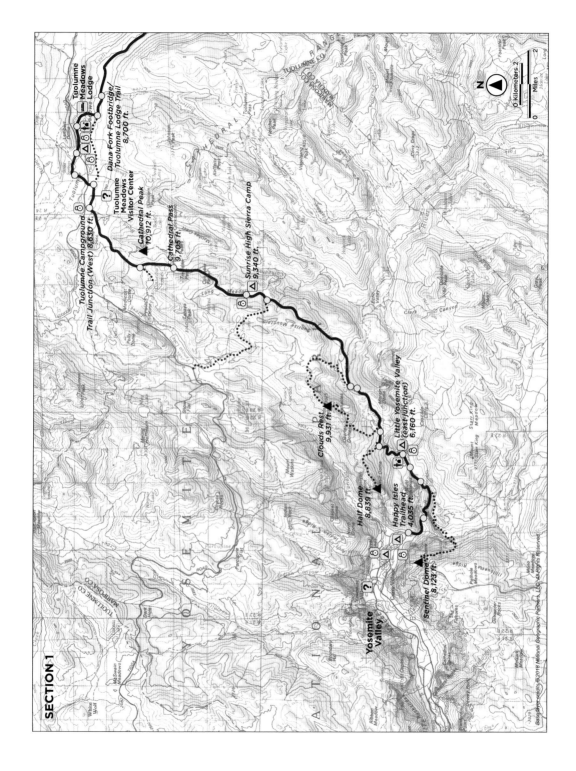

SECTION 1

Tuolumne Meadows Lodge

Tuolumne Meadows Lodge

Dana Fork Footbridge/
Tuolumne Lodge Trail
8,700 ft.

Tuolumne Meadows
Visitor Center

Tuolumne Campground
Trail Junction (West) 8,630 ft.

Cathedral Peak
10,912 ft.

Cathedral Pass
9,705 ft.

Sunrise High Sierra Camp
9,340 ft.

Clouds Rest
9,931 ft.

Little Yosemite Valley
(east junction)
6,160 ft.

Half Dome
8,839 ft.

Happy Isles
Trailhead
4,035 ft.

Yosemite
Valley

Sentinel Dome
8,123 ft.

N

0 Kilometers 2
0 Miles 2

MILEAGE MARKERS NORTH TO SOUTH

SECTION	TOTAL	ELEVATION	LANDMARK
0	0	4,035	Happy Isles Trailhead
1	1	4,540	Mist Trail Junction
3.7	3.7	5,995	Nevada Falls Bridge
4.3	4.3	6,140	Little Yosemite Valley (west junction)*
4.3	4.8	6,160	Little Yosemite Valley (east junction)*
6.1	6.1	7,010	Half Dome Trail
6.6	6.6	7,200	Clouds Rest Trail
8.5	8.5	8,010	Merced Lake Trail
8.6	8.6	8,070	Forsyth Trail
12.1	12.1	9,340	Sunrise High Sierra Camp*/Sunrise Lakes Trail
13	13	9,350	Echo Creek Trail
15.4	15.4	9,705	Cathedral Pass
16.2	16.2	9,450	Lower Cathedral Lake Trail
19.2	19.2	8,600	Cathedral Lakes Trailhead
20.1	20.1	8,630	Tuolumne Campground trail Junction (west)
20.6	20.6	8,600	Parsons Lodge/Soda Springs Jct
21.4	21.4	8,600	Lembert Dome Parking
22.2	22.2	8,700	Dana Fork Footbridge/Tuolumne Lodge Trail

*campground with bear boxes

ELEVATION PROFILE

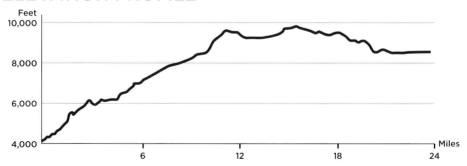

ALTERNATE TRAIL ACCESS POINTS

>> Glacier Point Trail to Little Yosemite Valley: 4.0 miles

>> Tenaya Lake to Sunrise Lakes Trail: 5.2 miles

INTRODUCTION

FRESH OFF AN APPALACHIAN TRAIL thru-hike and a move cross-country the following year from Connecticut at the age of 23, I immediately knew I wanted to leave the bustle of Los Angeles and return "home" to the mountains. My uncle and I decided to go full epic and backpack in the snowy Yosemite Valley during early March in order to take a peek at the start to the John Muir Trail. Snowshoes and winter gear packed, we set out not knowing what to expect, and that was the thrill of it. The unknown of a wilderness trip is what always leaves you craving more—you shall never know what's around that bend in the trail or over the next pass until you go there and see for yourself. We set out amid dark clouds that occasionally opened up to disperse patches of snowflakes along the trail. As we climbed steadily out of the valley floor with not a sound but our footsteps and the thundering Merced River and Vernal Falls, I was reminded of why this trail was envisioned, why it was created, and why is was named in honor of this great man, this Patriarch of the Sierra. I became one with John Muir that day and walked proud and mightily, rising foot by foot toward Little Yosemite Valley (LYV), passing Nevada Falls and having to put on snowshoes for the last 2 miles. We set up camp to the east of Half Dome in the LYV campground without a soul in sight that evening. A stunning glow from the moon reflected off the silent snow-covered terrain, inspiring dreams of completing the entire JMT someday.

Flash-forward fourteen years and I was back at the Happy Isles trailhead, but this time to start stitching together the trail I have been dreaming about ever since that soupy day on Mt. Katahdin and the silent winter night in Little Yosemite Valley. My life was completely different from that first time I stood at this trailhead. I had my beautiful and supportive wife, Crystalyn, at my side, with 8 days of food and snow gear on our backs, fully prepared to hike out of the overcrowded and flooded valley floor on a perfectly sunny and hot June day. The plan was to hike as far as we could toward the Cathedral Range, where the snow was rumored to be over 12 feet deep and the rivers screamed down to the valley floor like furious locomotives, already causing over a half a dozen deaths this season. Curious looks were tossed our way at every turn when tourists would catch sight of our bright-red snowshoes strapped to the exteriors of our packs. There wasn't a flake of snow in sight from the valley floor, and it was 85 degrees with naught a cloud in sight—we looked like total newbies. Little did they know what the terrain looked like another 13 miles up the trail, but we had prepared.

Earlier that year when I was applying for our JMT permits, it was a nerve-wracking period while we prayed we could get the dates we wanted in August when our work schedules allowed. We were lucky enough to win the lottery in our date range, with our starting trailhead being out of Tuolumne Meadows heading southbound. I figured this was a good situation since we would be able to get in a good "preparation" hike from Happy Isles to Tuolumne earlier in the season. Unfortunately for us, the snow

Alpine lily

Canyon dudleya

Fan-leafed cinquefoil

Lupine

Leichtlin's mariposa lily

Sierra daisy

Horsetail Firefall

never stopped falling that year, making it known as one of the wettest years on record for California, a mere two years after a record low.

This changed the whole trip when it came to preparation and logistics. We had to do a lot of research on forums to find out current snowpack levels and risks involved with the river crossings, hoping it would melt away by June when we had time for this first section. We no longer had the option to take the shuttle back to the valley from Tuolumne since parts of Tioga Road were still covered in 20+ feet of snow, 40-foot snowdrifts, and avalanche danger around every corner for the Caltrans crew cutting their way in from the east side of the pass.

Our packs were heavy—the climb is one of the longest on the entire trail—but our spirits were high, and my camera was ready to capture the Sierra Nevada in such a monumental year of weather. We encountered snow at the 8,200-foot level just past the Forsyth and Merced Lake Trail junctions. A combination of micro-spikes and snow-shoes, depending on the snow conditions in each area, helped get us to the southern edge of Long Meadow, where we made a nice snow camp at 9,600 feet elevation. The views to Matthes Crest and the Cathedral Range were ethereal—the snow went as far as the eye could see, giving the land an isolated feel. On top of that the last person we had seen was over 5 miles back, a stark contrast from the bright and sunny valley floor, which experienced multiple-hour traffic jams due to an overflow of visitors this season. This was as far as we would go for this trip; we didn't want to go too deep into the snow knowing there was a possible storm heading our way in the coming days. We enjoyed

An American Black Bear searches for berries near Little Yosemite Valley

the remainder of the trip on the side trails to the summit of Clouds Rest and into LYV. On June 11 a solid 3 inches of snow fell overnight on our final night camping at 6,000 feet, adding to the mystique of this record-breaking season.

OVERVIEW

Yosemite National Park is where it all begins. Here is where you can find the first steps of the legendary John Muir Trail, where John Muir first laid eyes on the Sierra Nevada range in 1868, now one of the most storied national parks in the world. When Theodore Solomons first envisioned the JMT at the ripe age of 14 in 1884, he wanted to walk along the entire chain of the majestic Sierra Crest, and it was in 1892 in Yosemite Valley where he also first began his explorations. It is quite appropriate the trail begins here, the valley for which John Muir battled nearly two decades of his life to save for future generations.

The trail between Yosemite Valley and Tuolumne Meadows is breathtaking in more ways than one. The stunning valley and waterfall views will spearhead ideas for more trips in the future, until the steep climb gets your blood pumping. Starting at the paved and crowded Happy Isles Trailhead, you will hike along and then above the Merced River, passing through the only stands of California black oak on the trail. Gray squirrels relish their meaty acorns surrounded by towering Douglas firs. Passing Vernal and Nevada Falls on your way to Little Yosemite Valley, you will climb over 2,000 feet, hugging switchbacks on the cliffside along the way. Stop and enjoy the view at the top of the thundering Nevada Falls, where a good majority of the day hikers will be turning around. After crossing a large bridge over the Merced River, you continue a short distance to LYV; there is excellent camping here if this is your destination for the day, with a nice trail into the side valley, the Cascade Cliffs, and Moraine Dome. LYV has a seasonal ranger station with toilets and food-storage lockers and plenty of camping spread out among the Jeffrey pines.

The next little section takes you up through more Jeffrey pines and stands of white firs as you ascend toward the trail junctions to Half Dome and then

RESUPPLY LOCATIONS

Yosemite National Park Post Office
Phone: (209) 372-4475
Mail packages to:

(Name)
c/o General Delivery
Yosemite National Park Post Office
9017 Village Dr.
Yosemite National Park, CA 95389
Arriving by: ETA

Tuolumne Meadows Post Office
Phone: (209) 372-8236
Mail packages to:

(Name)
c/o General Delivery
Tuolumne Meadows Post Office
14000 CA 120 East
Yosemite National Park, CA 95389
Arriving by: ETA

El Capitan and Half Dome in autumn

Looking down to the first footbridge
over the Merced River

PHOTOGRAPHY TIP: 📷
PHOTOGRAPHING MOVING WATER

Photographing waterfalls and streams can require some extra equipment and preparation to show the movement of water and give it a cottony flowing effect. The best time to photograph water is when there is cloud cover and diffused light, but if it is in the middle of the day with a lot of sunlight on the water, you may be required to use a neutral-density filter on your lens to help get that exposure dialed in. A waterfall that is half in the sun and half in the shade will be difficult to capture and is not the most ideal situation. Once you arrive at the location, be sure to walk around the area to locate the best spot for your photo. Shooting from the side of a waterfall can sometimes show a better angle than straight on. Also, the inclusion of foreground and background elements can improve the overall image.

Be sure to use a tripod and then set your camera to manual mode and the lowest ISO setting, and change your shutter speed to one-eighth of a second to 2 seconds and compensate by closing your aperture down to the smallest it will go, such as an f16 or f22. Using a remote, a plunger, or the timer will prevent any vibrations or movement of the camera. Try a variety of shots with different shutter speeds to see what you like best.

Sunrise Creek cascades through a burned section from the Meadow Fire of 2014

Clouds Rest—both are excellent and steep side trails, and if you find the time to do them, you will be rewarded with tremendous views of the valley. On the way you will hike along and cross Sunrise Creek, with stunning views of both granite formations along with the rounded summit of Mt. Starr King to the south. A multitude of camping options can be found along the creek. You will soon travel through a recently burned area of the park, where you can see an abundance of new life growing with vigor from the ashes. The trail then hikes along a ridge above LYV with views to the southeast of the glacier-carved domes and cliffs below and the magnificent Clark Range just beyond.

NO FEATURE, HOWEVER, OF ALL THE NOBLE LANDSCAPE AS SEEN FROM HERE SEEMS MORE WONDERFUL THAN THE CATHEDRAL [PEAK] ITSELF, A TEMPLE DISPLAYING NATURE'S BEST MASONRY AND SERMONS IN STONES.

—John Muir

From here you enter the steep terrain below Sunrise Mountain and climb up and over to the open and lush Long Meadow and the Sunrise High Sierra Camp, where you will find toilets and food-storage lockers as well as a variety of camping options. This is where you will really begin to see the abundance of wildflowers if you happen to be hiking during the main bloom. Look for the elegant Sierra lily and the simple Leichtlin's mariposa lily near damp sections. From the Sunrise High Sierra Camp, the trail ascends to Cathedral Pass (9,705 feet), where views of the Columbia Finger, Tresidder Peak, Cathedral Peak, Echo Peaks, and Matthes Crest dominate your view. As you descend to Tuolumne, be sure to stop at either Upper or Lower Cathedral

Geology Notes from Michael Hassan

When massive bodies of molten rock (like the ones that form much of the Sierra) solidify several miles underground, they are under enormous amounts of pressure caused by the mass of rock and soil sitting on top of them. As erosion takes effect and the material covering the now-solid granitic rocks is eroded away, the pressure on the rock gradually lessens, eventually causing the rock to expand when enough pressure is removed. Since granite tends to deform more brittlely (breaking, rather than bending), as it expands, sheets of rock between 1.5 and 30 feet thick begin to peel off the rock like layers of an onion. Some of the most notable pieces of the Sierra landscape that formed through this process are Half Dome and Liberty Cap in Yosemite Valley, Lembert Dome in Tuolumne Meadows, and countless other, smaller domes that are visible from the John Muir Trail as it exits Tuolumne Meadows.

*Moon over
Half Dome*
re-created in
LEGO
JAMES BANKS,
MASTER BUILDER

The first mile of the JMT
paved for all to access

Lake—the views are legendary, and many hikers choose to camp here for the stunning sunrise and sunset views across the lakes to Cathedral Peak. A little-known fact is that John Muir himself was the first to climb this unmistakable peak along its northwestern face back in 1869.

From the Cathedral Lakes region, the trail descends gently toward Tuolumne Meadows through mountain hemlocks and lodgepole pines with intermittent views to your northwest, first of Medlicott and Mariuolumne Domes, then Fairvew Dome as you get close to Tioga Road. Highway 120, Tioga Pass Road, was once known as Mono Trail and the Great Sierra Wagon Road, the main throughway for Native Americans to the land from the east to the west. After you cross Budd Creek on a footbridge, the

EXCERPTS FROM THE BACKCOUNTRY

Andrew Skurka – Adventurer, Guide, Speaker, Writer (andrewskurka.com)

I've always approached long-distance trails like the JMT from the perspective of an endurance athlete. Like other hikers, I'm drawn to the landscape, the simple existence, and the camaraderie of a group. But I also thoroughly enjoy—and seek out—the physical and emotional challenge of pushing hard for days or weeks at a time. How deep can I dig?

Some might argue that I'm not stopping to smell the roses when I cover 30+ miles in a day, or when I ascend Forrester Pass at midnight after getting over Pinchot and Glen hours earlier. But my experience has been just the opposite: When I'm at the limits of my endurance, I'm humbled and amazed most by my surroundings. It's as if the fatigue makes me extra vulnerable to the recognition of scale: It's giant and timeless, and I'm tiny and mortal.

Howie Schwartz – SMG Lead Guide & Owner, UIAGM/
IFMGA Ski and Mountain Guide (sierramtnguides.com)

The most profound change in the High Sierra is the retreat and demise of the glaciers, snowfields, and ice couloirs. Late-summer alpine ice climbing is virtually extinct, save for a couloir or two. The loss of ice within couloirs has exponentially increased the speed of snowmelt in these features. In the last five years, we have stopped guiding snow climbs from the Palisade Glacier by mid-July due to the dearth of snow and increase in size and frequency of rockfall. Rock underneath the seasonal snow causes melt from top and bottom, and once the snow melts away, the mountains begin to succumb to forces of water and gravity. Even after a record snow year, we expect that the tops of the high couloirs will melt out by mid- to late summer and they will become unsafe to climb. It is going to take many consecutive winters like that of 2016–'17 or many stormy, cold summers to bring back the ice and the glaciers.

Sparkle - Cathedral Peak
and star trails from Upper
Cathedral Lake JOSHUA CRIPPS

I HAVE SEEN THEM [SIERRA CHIPMUNKS] RUNNING ABOUT ON SHEER PRECIPICES OF THE YOSEMITE WALLS SEEMINGLY HOLDING ON WITH AS LITTLE EFFORT AS FLIES, AND AS UNCONSCIOUS OF DANGER, WHERE, IF THE SLIGHTEST SLIP WERE MADE, THEY WOULD HAVE FALLEN TWO OR THREE THOUSAND FEET. HOW FINE IT WOULD BE COULD WE MOUNTAINEERS CLIMB THESE TREMENDOUS CLIFFS WITH THE SAME SURE GRIP!

—John Muir

trail heads to the east and parallels the road for a mile before you have a choice to take a side trail to the campgrounds and store or you can continue on the JMT across the road into the open Tuolumne Meadows. As you hike through the meadows, you will pass the Parson's Memorial Lodge, a historic location that was built in 1915 as a meetinghouse and library for the Sierra Club. Just beyond the lodge is the old log structure protecting one of the main Soda Springs, where naturally occurring carbonated spring water comes from the earth. It was at this location that John Muir conceived the idea to turn the Yosemite Valley into a national park and protect it for generations to come.

As you pass Lembert Dome to the east, the trail crosses the road for the last time for the reminder of the JMT. Many hikers choose to get a resupply at the Tuolumne Meadows Store and eat a juicy burger before heading off into the wild. The store also has a variety of camping foods at a premium price, so if additional items are needed to supplement your journey, here is your opportunity. The Wilderness Center is also located here, where you can pick up permits if your journey starts here.

BEST CAMPSITE IN THIS SECTION

CATHEDRAL LAKES

The Cathedral Lakes area is absolutely breathtaking, especially considering it is so accessible from Tioga Road in Tuolumne Meadows. Attaining a permit to camp here can prove to be difficult during the summer months, but as long as the road is open, all seasons here can be incredible. The sunsets and sunrises from these lakes are timeless and will stay with you forever. There is also incredible access to Cathedral Peak and its entire range from here if you feel inclined to climb one of the many routes available. Watch for the ducks that inhabit the lakes—you can spot them diving down to the bottom to feed in the shallower sections. Be sure to pick your site carefully as the vegetation around the lakes constitutes a very fragile ecological environment and the smallest damage can be irreversible.

SECTION 2
TUOLUMNE MEADOWS TO RED'S MEADOW

Gateway to the High Sierra

Sunrise in Lyell Canyon

Approaching Donahue Pass in the early winter

SECTION 2
TUOLUMNE MEADOWS TO RED'S MEADOW

LOCATION: Yosemite National Park, Ansel Adams Wilderness, Devils Postpile National Monument, Inyo National Forest

LENGTH: 37.7 miles

ELEVATION GAIN/ LOSS (NORTH -> SOUTH): +7,190 ft./ −8,105 ft.

LOWEST POINT: Rainbow Falls Trail, 7,470 ft.

HIGHEST POINT: Donahue Pass, 11,055 ft.

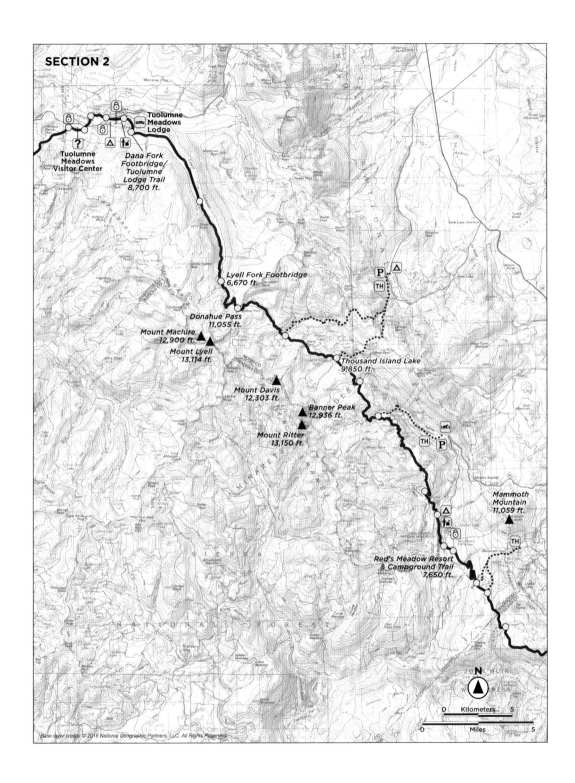

SECTION 2

Tuolumne Meadows Lodge

Tuolumne Meadows Visitor Center

Dana Fork Footbridge/Tuolumne Lodge Trail 8,700 ft.

Lyell Fork Footbridge 6,670 ft.

Donahue Pass 11,055 ft.

Mount Maclure 12,900 ft.

Mount Lyell 13,114 ft.

Mount Davis 12,303 ft.

Banner Peak 12,936 ft.

Mount Ritter 13,150 ft.

Thousand Island Lake 9,850 ft.

Mammoth Mountain 11,059 ft.

Red's Meadow Resort & Campground Trail 7,650 ft.

N

Kilometers
0   5

Miles
0   5

MILEAGE MARKERS NORTH TO SOUTH

SECTION	TOTAL	ELEVATION	LANDMARK
0	22.2	8,700	Dana Fork Footbridge/Tuolumne Lodge Trail
1	23.2	8,660	Lyell Fork Footbridge/Tuolumne Campground Trail (east)*
1.5	23.7	8,730	Rafferty Creek Trail
5.7	27.9	8,890	Vogelsang Pass Trail
9.7	31.9	9,670	Lyell Fork Footbridge
13.5	35.7	11,055	Donahue Pass
16.8	39	9,630	Rush Creek Trail
19.9	42.1	9,850	Thousand Island Lake
22.4	44.6	9,690	Garnet Lake
25.8	48	8,770	Shadow Lake & Footbridge
33.9	56.1	8,125	Johnston Meadow/Minaret Creek Trail
34.3	56.5	7,685	Devils Postpile National Monument Boundary
36.5	58.7	7,470	Rainbow Falls Trail
37.7	59.9	7,650	Red's Meadow Resort & Campground Trail*

*campground with bear boxes

ELEVATION PROFILE

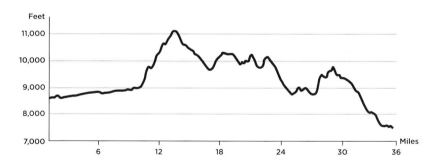

ALTERNATE TRAIL ACCESS POINTS

>> Rush Creek Trail to Rush Creek Trailhead – 8.7 miles

>> Thousand Island Lake to Rush Creek Trailhead – 6.5 miles

>> Shadow Lake to Agnew Meadow Trailhead – 4.2 miles

INTRODUCTION

AT THE END OF OCTOBER 2016, my wife and I decided to take a training trip from Tuolumne Meadows to Red's Meadow. The weather report had shown two rainstorms predicted for that week, but we knew there was at least a day and a half of good weather to get us over Donahue Pass. We hired Rolf Knutsen, shuttle service owner, who picked us up in Mammoth and drove us to the Tuolumne Meadows wilderness center, where around 2 p.m. we started the journey on a warm and clear day. Covering a little over 6.5 miles of mellow terrain before sunset, we decided to camp out on a beautiful spot near the Lyell Fork.

The morning sky was bright and sunny above us, with dark clouds looming over Mt. Lyell, the highest point in Yosemite. Around 1 o'clock a light drizzle started coming from the clouds, and we continued to hike for a mile and a half until the sky opened up on us around 10,000 feet in elevation. There was a mad dash to unpack the tent and get all the gear and ourselves into the dry cocoon we would be trapped in until this storm let up. The rain worsened as time passed that afternoon, coming in waves of torrential downpour, patches of pea-size hail, and teasing us sporadically with periods of no precipitation at all. We were forced to cook dinner in the vestibule of our tent that evening as the rain continued and the temperatures slowly dropped. We had a bad feeling about the following day.

The next day we awoke to gray clouds and the all-too-familiar pitter-patter of rain on the roof. Our hearts sank as we realized we might lose an entire day, along with an unnerving feeling that Donahue Pass, another 1,000 feet above us, was likely getting caked in snow. We passed the time with word games, books, and lots of snacking. The temperature dropped as the hours passed, bringing louder thumps to the rain fly of our tent. I poked my head outside to see what was going on and was greeted

KEEP CLOSE TO NATURE'S HEART … AND BREAK CLEAR AWAY, ONCE IN AWHILE, AND CLIMB A MOUNTAIN OR SPEND A WEEK IN THE WOODS. WASH YOUR SPIRIT CLEAN.

—John Muir

with a huge blob of sleet to my face. Soon enough the sleet turned to snow flurries, covering our campsite with a thin wintry layer. As the light in the sky began to fade, signaling sunset, the snow also began to cease as the thick clouds finally parted above us, revealing clear skies in all directions! Huzzah! It was time to take some pictures! After a grueling 26 hours of being tent-bound, it was nice to finally step outside and breathe the fresh air without struggling to stay dry. I decided to scramble 200 feet up the granite slabs to our east and was greeted by the freshly snowcapped mountains basking in the majestic Sierra alpenglow.

Red mountain heather

Mountain prettyface

Sierra penstemon

Sierra stickseed

Swamp onion

Western wallflower

Banner Peak reflected
from Island Pass

The next morning we faced snow just a few minutes from camp, and donning our micro-spikes, we pushed on toward the pass. As the snow got deeper and we post-holed up to our thighs, we had officially lost the trail around the 10,600-foot range, just as the gusts of wind and snow began whipping us in the face. Crystalyn and I took a long break in a protected patch of lodgepoles to enjoy the view. My wife wrote in her journal that evening: "The wind was sharp and unfriendly, and if not for erasing our trail, it really otherwise wouldn't have stood a chance against us. The vast beauty and solitude of that moment, and others like it, is what makes life worth living!"

We decided not to risk it and made the safe choice to turn back and retreat to Tuolumne Meadows. We knew another storm was coming and if the first storm left this much snow, we didn't want to be trapped at this elevation by another one. By four o'clock we had made it all the way back to Lyell Canyon, picked a campsite, and

RESUPPLY LOCATIONS

Red's Meadow Resort, Campground & Store
For payment & shipping info: www
.redsmeadow.com
Phone: (760) 934-2345
Mail packages to:

(Your Name)
Red's Meadow Resort
PO Box 395
Mammoth Lakes, CA 93546

Mammoth Lakes Post Office
Phone: (760) 934-2205
Mail packages to:

(Your Name)
c/o General Delivery
Mammoth Lakes Post Office
Mammoth Lakes, CA 93546
Arriving by: ETA

Geology Notes from Michael Hassan

Just north of Red's Meadow lies Devils Postpile National Monument. Devils Postpile is a basalt outcrop that formed between 80 million and 100 million years ago. Several miles north of where the monument now stands, a volcanic vent began spewing exceptionally hot basaltic lava that flowed toward Red's Meadow until it was stopped by a natural dam—perhaps made of glacially deposited rocks. This created a lake of lava that was over 400 feet deep in some areas. As the flow subsided and the lava began to cool, it contracted because basalt's liquid volume is greater than its solid volume. The outcrop remained concealed until glaciers excavated the formation over several discrete periods—most recently just 15,000 years ago.

Early winter sunset in Lyell Canyon

enjoyed a gorgeous sunset on the high summits we had just left with nary a cloud in sight.

At some point well into the night, it started to rain and we awoke to the 2-inch puddle of water our tent was sitting in, along with our shoes, hiking socks, and packs. My wife and I quickly got up to move the tent to another spot and watched as the rain persisted and temperatures began to drop, once again transforming the rain into sleet and within a couple hours, gargantuan snowflakes, blanketing the entire canyon in silence. It was another day of snacks, word games, snacks, books, snacks, naps . . . you get the idea. The snow didn't stop until the middle of the night when the stars and Milky Way finally revealed themselves.

After donning our newly frozen hiking shoes in the morning, we started hiking in 18 inches of fresh snow toward Tuolumne Meadows. The trickiest part was crossing Ireland Creek, which had surged in width three-fold since we had initially crossed it just a few days prior. It took some time to discover a safe location to cross—a snow-covered log roughly 2 feet in diameter 8 feet above the coursing creek—and needless to say it was exciting. We covered the soaking-wet final miles to Tuolumne Meadows quickly, knowing we could use the payphones to call Rolf for a ride. When we arrived at the first payphone, it was dead, and upon arrival to Tioga Road, we saw no sign of human life or traffic. We knew the gate must have been closed and we were stranded in the park. That evening the clouds rolled in thick just after sunset and the snow came down again, dropping another 6 inches.

The following morning I did a reconnaissance mission to the lodge to see if I could find a working payphone. Eventually I found two more, but both were not working. It was at this point I realized we would have to make the 20-mile journey on foot down Tioga Road to Lee Vining, where we could then call for a ride to Mammoth. Upon my arrival back at camp, Crystalyn informed me she just saw a snowplow go up the road! I jumped with joy and waited at the road until I saw it return an hour later. The driver stopped and he confirmed the gate was closed and my wife and I would have to walk 20 miles back to Lee Vining. I asked if he would kindly send a message to our family to inform them that we were safe and would return a day or two late. He kindly obliged and took down the information. To our fortune he offered to make a CB radio call to the valley to see if any park rangers were available to assist us. Fifteen minutes later we got a reply that a ranger would be on his way. The first-year Yosemite ranger kindly gave us a ride all the way down Tioga Road into Lee Vining, where we secured a warm, dry hotel room for the evening and dined on hefty cheeseburgers.

Banner Peak lights up with sunrise at
Thousand Island Lake

Sunset colors on
Thousand Island Lake

PHOTOGRAPHY TIP: BLACK-AND-WHITE PHOTOGRAPHY BY PETER ESSICK, NATIONAL GEOGRAPHIC PHOTOGRAPHER

The Sierra high country that makes up most of the John Muir Trail is well suited for black-and-white photography. From the deep forests to mountain lakes and especially the glacier-polished granite landscapes above the tree line, the elemental forms are accentuated without the distraction of color. I don't think that it is a coincidence that Ansel Adams found this wilderness region to be the perfect subject matter to express an emotional fondness for nature through the medium of black-and-white photography almost one hundred years ago.

It is still possible to make expressive black-and-white photographs with today's digital cameras. It is best to capture the image in RGB color and then convert the image into black and white using an image-processing software program such as Adobe Photoshop. This provides the most control over how various colors will be represented in tones of gray, similar to the way that color filters were once used when photographing with black-and-white film. It is also best to set the LCD monitor on your camera to monotone so you can see what the image will look like in black and white at the time of image capture.

Photographing in black and white should change your approach. Look for scenes with dramatic contrast and lighting. The granite boulders and faces lend themselves to creative compositions, but the dark metamorphic rocks of the Minaret range can also form elegant lines against the skyline. The afternoon sun reflections off lakes and ice work well in black and white, as well as time exposures of moving water at dawn or dusk. Afternoon storms, which are more common in the late summer, can create dramatic images with the contrast of the thunderclouds and patches of sunlight painting a chiaroscuro effect across the Sierra high country.

Afternoon thunderstorm,
Garnet Lake
PETER ESSICK

OVERVIEW

This 33.4-mile section starts at Tuolumne Meadows; this is where most thru-hikers will get their first resupply after starting in Yosemite Valley at Happy Isles. The start of the hike is very beautiful travel over a series of wooden bridges across the Lyell Fork into the thicker forest as you work your way into the heart of Lyell Canyon. The trailhead and first couple miles can quickly get crowded with day-hikers and tourists during the summer months, so it's best to scurry into the heart of the canyon.

I'D RATHER BE IN THE MOUNTAINS THINKING OF GOD, THAN IN CHURCH THINKING ABOUT THE MOUNTAINS.

—John Muir

There are many excellent camping spots along the hike through the canyon as the mountains rise higher and higher on your flanks. You must camp at least 4 miles from the main road, but you will find nice spots near many of the side trails such as the Parker Pass Trail and the Evelyn Lake/Vogelsang Pass Trail. Once you arrive at the Lyell Fork base trail, the elevation begins

EXCERPTS FROM THE BACKCOUNTRY

John Sutter: The award-winning columnist for CNN spent three weeks kayaking and walking down the San Joaquin River to the San Francisco Bay with expert guide Darin McQuoid. (www.johndsutter.com)

The memory that most sticks with me is one I used to end my CNN article on the San Joaquin: Darin and I were walking along a fork of the river on the way to Thousand Island Lake. I heard the water rumbling below and remarked that the river, to me, "sounds like a highway." He didn't miss a beat. "Highways sound like rivers," he said. This was my first encounter with what I've come to think of as a river-first mind-set. We modern people have learned much, but we have lost our connection to the natural world. We don't understand the environment as we once did. We don't know where rivers start, where they end, what happens in between. We don't know their stories, and we don't know why they matter—to us, to fish, to the food we eat and grow. This is terribly troubling to me. And Darin's river-first way of seeing the world—a view that not only includes natural systems but starts with them and realizes their central importance in all that we do—actually helped rewire my brain. When my tandem kayak floated under the Golden Gate Bridge about three weeks later, at the end of my journey down the San Joaquin and into the San Francisco Bay, I heard the roar of traffic on the bridge above me. My first thought was "Highways sound like rivers." I still think that way now.

Shadow Creek flows down
from Ediza Lake

I AM LOSING PRECIOUS DAYS. I AM DEGENERATING INTO A MACHINE FOR MAKING MONEY. I AM LEARNING NOTHING IN THIS TRIVIAL WORLD OF MEN. I MUST BREAK AWAY AND GET OUT INTO THE MOUNTAINS TO LEARN THE NEWS.

—*John Muir*

to gain quickly. After navigating switchbacks for a couple miles, the terrain evens out a little as you come up to the Lyell Forks Bridge, which offers excellent camping options.

From here the trail climbs to the Upper Lyell Headwaters just above 10,000 feet, where there is more excellent camping along the creek on the slabs. The trail continues to climb to Donahue Pass, where the terrain is breathtaking and you will find yourself next to one of California's largest glaciers, the Lyell Glacier, to your west. Take a quick side trip up to the summit of Donahue Peak if you have the energy reserves—you won't regret it for the stunning views of Yosemite's high country.

A storm approaches the Lyell Range and Donahue Pass DAMON CORSO

Snow camping along the JMT

The outlet of Garnet Lake

After conquering Donahue Pass you officially leave Yosemite National Park and enter into the Ansel Adams Wilderness, where you will spend the next 5 miles walking on the eastern side of the great Sierra Crest, whose waters drain into the Mono Lake Basin. The trail descends via switchback with a beautiful lush landscape littered with glacial slabs and boulders, dropping you down toward the Thousand Island Lakes basin. After descending a few miles, you will come to the junction of the Rush Creek Trail. If you need an emergency resupply, you can access the town June Lake from here.

From this trail junction you moderately climb up to Island Pass, where you are rewarded with stunning 360-degree views and a few small tarns. You will finally descend from here to the stunning Thousand Island Lake. There is lots of good camping around this picturesque region, although no camping is allowed within a quarter mile of the lake outlet. But you are sure to find a secluded spot along the northern or southern shores. From here the trail passes Emerald and Ruby Lakes on the way to the serene Garnet Lake, which is very similar to Thousand Island Lake, with its tiny islands scattered across its body. Over the next 4 miles, you lose 1,000 feet in elevation

Rainbow Falls

on the hike toward the Shadow Lake Junction. There is no camping allowed here, but it is a beautiful location for a lunch break or a quick swim.

A short ascent brings you to Rosalie Lake and finally to the long descent into Red's Meadow and Devils Postpile National Monument, where your next resupply point is. The scenery changes drastically over the next 9 miles as you descend lower and lower to 7,650 feet at Red's Meadow. You can see destruction to the massive trees from the 2011 Devils Windstorm, which brought winds upward of 200 mph to the area, and the 1992 Rainbow Fire, which had previously devastated the area. If you have the time to add an extra mile or two, navigate your way first past the geologic phenomenon Devils Postpile, explained in greater detail earlier in this chapter, and then continue on to Rainbow Falls, where you can enjoy two very stunning and different natural landmarks of the area.

BEST CAMPSITE IN THIS SECTION

THOUSAND ISLAND LAKE

This is one of the most recognizable lakes in the Ansel Adams Wilderness and is known for being one of Adams's favorite places to photograph. Banner and Ritter Peaks tower over the tree-covered islands and make for incredible scenery. This is a good spot to spend the day eating lunch and swimming out to the islands if you can handle the temperatures. Plan on arriving earlier in the day to snag a campsite and enjoy all that the lake has to offer. Camping is not allowed within a quarter mile of the outlet—be sure to follow the use trail around the northern edge of the lake to excellent camping among the scattered patches of grass and sandy slabs.

Because Thousand Island Lake is so iconic and well known, it can be crowded. If you can't find a suitable campsite here, head south to Ruby Lake, which rests in an incredible granite basin with great campsites too.

SECTION 3
RED'S MEADOW TO MUIR TRAIL RANCH

The John Muir Wilderness

The Minarets and Ritter Range
grab the first light

An ocean of granite awaits as the trail approcahes Duck Creek

SECTION 3
RED'S MEADOW TO MUIR TRAIL RANCH

LOCATION: Ansel Adams Wilderness, Devils Postpile National Monument, Inyo National Forest, Sierra National Forest, John Muir Wilderness

LENGTH: 46.3 miles

ELEVATION GAIN/ LOSS (NORTH -> SOUTH): +11,610ft/ –10,910 ft.

LOWEST POINT: Red's Meadow Resort & Campground Trail, 7,650 ft.

HIGHEST POINT: Silver Pass, 10,900 ft.

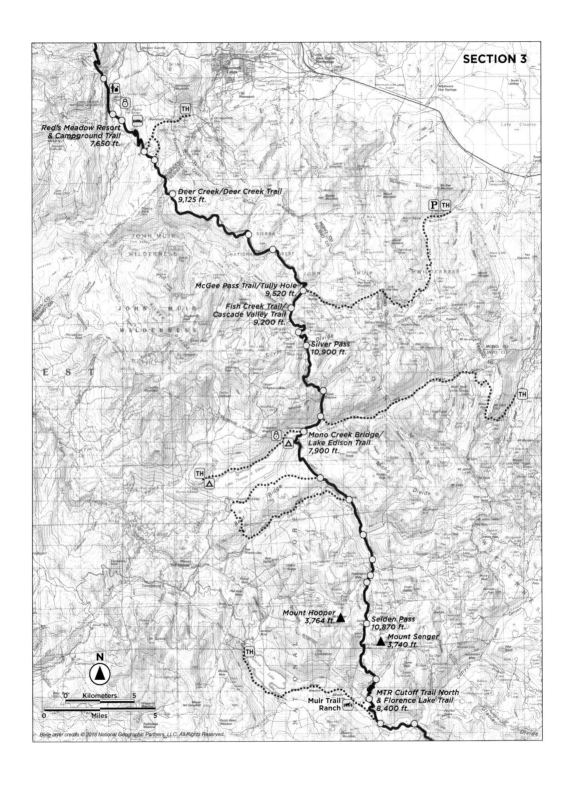

Red's Meadow Resort
& Campground Trail
7,650 ft.

Deer Creek/Deer Creek Trail
9,125 ft.

McGee Pass Trail/Tully Hole
9,520 ft.

Fish Creek Trail/
Cascade Valley Trail
9,200 ft.

Silver Pass
10,900 ft.

Mono Creek Bridge/
Lake Edison Trail
7,900 ft.

Mount Hooper
3,764 ft.

Selden Pass
10,870 ft.

Mount Senger
3,740 ft.

Muir Trail
Ranch

MTR Cutoff Trail North
& Florence Lake Trail
8,400 ft.

N

Kilometers
0   5

Miles
0   5

Base layer credits © 2016 National Geographic Partners, LLC. All Rights Reserved.

MILEAGE MARKERS NORTH TO SOUTH

SECTION	TOTAL	ELEVATION	LANDMARK
0	59.9	7,650	Red's Meadow Resort & Campground Trail*
2.9	62.8	8,670	Mammoth Pass Trail (north)
3.7	63.6	8,910	Mammoth Pass Trail (south)
5.5	65.4	9,125	Deer Creek/Deer Creek Trail
9.9	69.8	10,150	Duck Creek/Duck Pass Trail
11.9	71.8	9,930	Purple Lake
15.8	75.7	9,520	McGee Pass Trail/Tully Hole
16.8	76.7	9,200	Fish Creek Trail/Cascade Valley Trail
19.1	79	10,525	Goodale Pass Trail
19.9	79.8	10,900	Silver Pass
23.5	83.4	9,005	Mott Lake Trail/N. Fork Mono Creek
24.7	84.6	8,330	Mono Creek Trail to Mono Pass
26	85.9	7,900	Mono Creek Bridge/Lake Edison Trail*
30	89.9	9,900	Bear Ridge Trail
31.8	91.7	8,930	Bear Creek Trail
33.7	93.6	9,305	Lake Italy Trail
34.9	94.8	9,550	Bear Creek/Seven Gables Trail
35.9	95.8	10,010	Sandpiper Lake Trail/Rosemarie Meadow
36.1	96	10,025	Rose Lake Trail
38.6	98.5	10,870	Selden Pass
42.6	102.5	9,720	Senger Creek Crossing
44.6	104.5	8,400	MTR Cutoff Trail North & Florence Lake Trail
46.3	106.2	7,900	MTR Cutoff Trail South & Florence Lake Trail

*campground with bear boxes

HOW GLORIOUS A GREETING THE SUN
GIVES THE MOUNTAINS!

—*John Muir*

INTRODUCTION

LITTLE DID I KNOW WHEN HIKING OUT OF RED'S MEADOW that I would be facing one of my biggest challenges physically and mentally on the entire trail. In my head I was still that spry 22-year-old who consistently cranked out 25-to-30-mile days on the Appalachian Trail, but in reality I was nearing 40 and took much longer to recover from adventures like this. I had managed to keep my hiking strengths in tune over the years through rock climbing, mountaineering, and just doing my highly physical job as an adventure photographer, but my body was not prepared for what my mind and heart wanted to do on this trail.

Nearly every day I found something extra to do just off the JMT that led me to a perfect spot for photos. I am the type to

> ONE MAY FANCY THE CLOUDS THEMSELVES ARE PLANTS, SPRINGING UP IN THE SKY-FIELDS AT THE CALL OF THE SUN, GROWING IN BEAUTY UNTIL THEY REACH THEIR PRIME, SCATTERING RAIN AND HAIL LIKE BERRIES AND SEEDS, THEN WILTING AND DYING.
>
> —*John Muir*

ELEVATION PROFILE

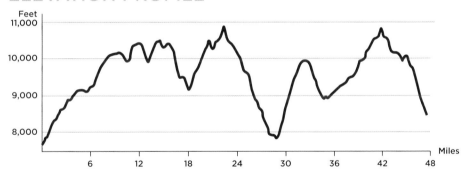

ALTERNATE TRAIL ACCESS POINTS

>> Mammoth Pass Trail North Junction – 3.1 miles

>> Mammoth Pass Trail South Junction – 3.5 miles

>> McGee Pass Trail – 13.6 miles

>> Mono Creek & Mono Pass Trail – 14.6 miles

>> Lake Edison Trail – 6.0 miles

>> Bear Ridge Trail – 5.0 miles

>> Bear Creek Trail – 8.6 miles

>> Florence Lake Trail – 7.8 miles

Grey-crowned Rosy Finch

always wonder what the view is just over the next ridge, and I don't regret any of these extra hikes or climbs that tacked miles and thousands of extra feet to my journey—the photos and memories are priceless. Over my first 15 days I went everywhere my heart desired: climbed Cathedral Peak and the Columbia Finger in Tuolumne, visited Ediza Lake nuzzled beneath the Minarets and Ritter Range, labored the wrong way up the Red Cones late in the evening to sleep under the stars, and lastly climbed steep fifth-class terrain to the summit of Mt. Senger, where the views from its 12,286-foot summit were incomparable and far superior than the ones I found below at Selden Pass.

It was that final day, summiting Mt. Senger early in the morning, that really put my body and mind to the test. I descended back to my camp at Marie Lake; with plenty of sun left, I realized I could make it to Muir Trail Ranch (MTR) before the end of the day if I hustled. I packed up quickly as a mass of portentous storm clouds rolled in from the north. I hiked through marshy terrain between my backcountry campsite and the JMT to begin the short climb to Selden Pass. On the opposite side of the pass, the clouds unfastened their hold of the rain and sent a volley of thunderclaps to chase me away from photographing a large bloom of mountaineer shooting stars along Sallie Keyes Creek. I hastened my pace and descended through beautiful scenery past Heart Lake and Sallie Keyes Lakes on a beeline to the MTR.

As I made my way down the final steep descent, out of the grasp of the passing tempest, I could no longer ignore the sharp throb in both big toes; I walked more cautiously as trail conditions deteriorated into an infuriating pile of small, sharp rocks.

A foraging Stellar's Jay

Pacfic Chorus Frog

A curious Pika in a high elevation talus field

Crimson columbine

Alpine columbine

Little elephant's-head

Monkey flower

Paintbrush

Ranger's buttons

After a storm at Lake Virginia

To keep my mind off the pain, I calculated my elevation loss for the day, realizing that once I got to the ranch, I would have descended over 5,000 feet. Soon enough the bones in my feet and legs started to hurt from all the pounding on rocky terrain. I began to second-guess what my next step on this trail was going to be. Was one zero day going to be enough to recover, or would I have to take a whole week off and risk not finishing within my permit time line? I really wasn't sure what the answer was. I just knew that I had to get to the ranch before dark, get some food in me, and rest.

When I arrived at MTR, I ran into my new friend Caymin. Both of us were broken in spirit and body. He similarly didn't know if he was going to be able to continue from this point on. Not only were we both disheartened by our current ailments, but also the thought of leaving MTR with 11 days of food to get to Mt. Whitney was already giving my lower back angst. We decided we should sleep on it and convene in the morning on our day off.

That morning we both awoke late and had breakfast together in the sun along the San Joaquin; we made small talk, mostly to avoid the major issues at hand. Around noon we made the short walk over to the ranch to collect our resupply buckets and

Andrew Bentz getting some turns in
alone in the Sierra Nevada
ANDREW BENTZ

reassess our situations. Hopefully a package from home would turn the tide in our favor. A fresh bottle of bourbon showed up in Caymin's bucket, and after making some new friends, trading and eating lots of food, we found a nice spot to kick back and have some sips of this lovely elixir. As the afternoon progressed, we got to discussing what optional exit trails lay ahead if we needed to bail early for more rest and recovery. This was the first step to negate the thought of getting off the trail.

NO PAIN HERE. NO DULL EMPTY HOURS. NO FEAR OF THE PAST. NO FEAR OF THE FUTURE. THESE BLESSED MOUNTAINS ARE SO COMPACTLY FILLED WITH GOD'S BEAUTY NO PETTY PERSONAL HOPE OR EXPERIENCE HAS ROOM TO BE.

—*John Muir*

One long soak in the San Joaquin River, two hot meals, three shots of bourbon, and a reminder from one of John Muir's unsullied verses, and I realized there was no getting off the trail now.

The tides had shifted in less than 24 hours. My heart and soul were on board and urged by the draw to trek onward to the next locations I had been waiting months to experience, Evolution and Palisade Basins. I was relieved to hear Caymin had a similar change of heart and decided to forge onward as well. I walked tall, strong, and proud the next day, covering close to 15 miles with the most weight I would carry the entire trip, my efforts being rewarded with the most astonishing sunsets reflected onto the Evolution Creek cascade a stone's throw away from my secluded camp.

OVERVIEW

Upon leaving Red's Meadow Resort, you will hike through more pumice stone on your way through the scarred Rainbow Fire Area. Because there are no more trees left in this area, the views of Iron Mountain to the west are quite spectacular. You'll notice the variety of wildflowers near the seeps and small streams. Keep your eyes open for the bright-yellow primrose monkey flower, and you will also run across gooseberries, lupines, and sagebrush. As the trail steepens, you hike along switchbacks into the dense covering of western white and Jeffrey pines along with western junipers. The ascent will take you to the Mammoth Pass Trail junction and the base of the Red Cones. A hike to one of their summits is worth your effort as views north to the Ritter Range and the Minarets are absolutely beautiful.

Another trail to Mammoth Pass lies just ahead as you pass through Upper Crater Meadow, which will be full of wildflowers during the right time of year. The trail eases up as you arrive at the footbridge across Deer Creek and prepare for the next ascent to Duck Creek. A dry lodgepole-and-sagebrush forest emerges as you crest around to

Close encounter with a
6-point Mule Deer

the southern slopes. You will notice the change in rock more dramatically here. The landscape opens up surrounded by granite as you arrive at the Duck Pass Junction and the footbridge over Duck Creek.

Your eye will be drawn south to the dramatic Silver Divide as you continue along the trail toward Purple Lake and then the picturesque Lake Virginia, a wonderful subalpine region in which to camp or spend the afternoon. Take some time to wander around the lake to watch the wildlife play, and keep your eyes peeled for the vibrant Lemmon's Indian paintbrushes. A steep and exposed descent into Tully Hole leads you to a beautiful hike along Fish Creek to a large footbridge; there are some great campsites along the creek if you plan on staying at a lower elevation.

A steep climb out of the valley toward Silver Pass brings you through a thick forest of lodgepole pine and hemlock where black-eyed juncos will be flying around. You will cross lots of seeps and small creeks where crimson columbine and mountain bluebells flourish. As you ascend around to the southern side of the slope, the terrain gets rockier and drier as the view to the Great Silver Divide opens up. Squaw Lake sits just ahead in a little cirque. A short climb will take you to Chief Lake, with striking

Looking down to the Marie Lake basin
from atop Senger Peak

scenery in all directions and excellent camping options. You are sure to catch an amazing sunset here.

A short hike takes you to Silver Pass at 10,900 feet—the many lakes you can see from here are outstanding. On the south side of the pass, you walk through wide-open meadows along the edge of Silver Pass Lake, slowly descending toward Mono Creek. Towering granite monoliths ring the surroundings as you begin the steeper descent along Silver Pass Creek. Be sure to stop and enjoy the beautiful cascade just before the junction with the Mott Lakes Trail and the North Fork of Mono Creek. The trail follows beautiful slabs as the creek flows down to the junction with the Lake Edison Trail and a footbridge across the water with many fine campsites. The side trail to the Lake Edison boat ferry will take you to the dock, where you can catch a ride to Vermillion Valley Resort and get resupplied. There is also a trail around the north edge of the lake to the resort.

A steep climb up Bear Ridge will take you through a dense lodgepole forest. As you climb, western white pines and white firs begin to dominate the tree population. Passing trail junctions back down Bear Ridge to Lake Edison, the trail wraps around to excellent views south

RESUPPLY LOCATIONS

Vermillion Valley Resort at Edison Lake
For payment & shipping info: www.edison lake.com
Mail packages to:

(Your name and expected arrival date)
Vermillion Valley Resort
c/o Rancheria Garage
62311 Huntington Lake Rd.
Lakeshore, CA 93634

Muir Trail Ranch (MTR)
For payment and shipping info: www.muir trailranch.com
Mail packages to:

(Your name and expected arrival date)
c/o Muir Trail Ranch
PO Box 176
Lakeshore, CA 93634

PHOTOGRAPHY TIP: ASTROPHOTOGRAPHY BY DARK SKY PHOTOGRAPHY

Fast lenses and a handheld timer that will allow for exposure times greater than 30 seconds are a DSLR astrophotographer's greatest assets. For any given lens, the lower the f-stop, the more light will be captured during each exposure. Using a high ISO such as 1600 or 3200, or even higher on some newer cameras, will also produce more detail with shorter exposure times, but ultimately, the duration of the shot should always be maximized. When shooting on a static tripod (not tracking the sky), the wider the focal length, the longer the exposures can be before star trails occur. With a 15mm lens, an exposure time of 45 seconds might be fine, whereas with a 300mm lens, it may only take a few seconds before the stars begin to trail. Of course, sometimes trails are desired! When including devices, which allow the camera to track the sky, these rules can largely be thrown out the window, and a wide range of settings can be used, as exposure times are able to exceed several minutes. As with all photography, trial and error is the best recipe for success.

The Milky Way hangs over Heart Lake viewed from Selden Pass along the John Muir Trail
DARK SKY PHOTOGRAPHY

The last sunburst at Chief Lake

of Mt. Hooper, Seven Gables, and Mt. Senger. Shortly after, you will cross the Hilgard Fork and the main fork of Bear Creek—both can be troublesome in the early spring. As the climb continues the forest thins out and granite peaks and outcroppings take their place on the way to lush Rosemarie Meadows. Wonderful camping can be found just beyond the meadow at Marie Lake, a smaller and less crowded version of Thousand Island Lake.

The narrow summit of Selden Pass affords excellent views north to Marie Lake and the surrounding peaks, while to the south lie wildflower-rich meadows and a small stream leading to Heart Lake. Some of the species found here are rock fringe tucked into shady nooks, Sierra daisy just off the side of the trail, and granite gilia along the

ONE DAY'S EXPOSURE TO MOUNTAINS IS BETTER THAN CARTLOADS OF BOOKS. SEE HOW WILLINGLY NATURE POSES HERSELF UPON PHOTOGRAPHERS' PLATES. NO EARTHLY CHEMICALS ARE SO SENSITIVE AS THOSE OF THE HUMAN SOUL.

—*John Muir*

EXCERPTS FROM THE BACKCOUNTRY

Andrew Bentz – Long-Distance Hiker, Second-Fastest Known Time (FKT) Unsupported on JMT, Trans-Sierra Skier

I remember having an instant connection to the Sierra Nevada. Ever since my first backpacking trip when I was 11, it all just felt right and made sense to me. I was pretty spoiled to have it all so close. I have always been fascinated with pushing myself in the backcountry setting, and in the winter the Sierra turns into my playground. I assess the risk and if I feel good about it, I can just keep going. I remember one day I skied the equivalent of 50 miles on the Sierra High Route (SHR), from before light in the morning to after dark. I was moving for nearly 20 hours with almost no breaks. A lot of it is just me being antsy and wanting to get more miles in, but it seems to me that the longer I move, and the harder I push, the more satisfied I will be with myself at the end of the day. At the end of that day, I was heading down to French Canyon, just zooming across the icy lakes and hard snow yelling and making weird noises. Having so much fun, I felt so alive and the day felt so full. The Sierra is a place where you can still come and have a pure "backcountry experience."

Herb Rickert – JMT & PCT Thru-Hikes in the 1950s, Sierra Explorer, Santa Barbara Rock-Climbing Pioneer

Waking up to the moon rising, or going and keeping right on hiking after sunset, those are charming experiences. I did a lot of hiking by moonlight so I could go with minimum gear; I tried to design different sleeping gear—the idea was to make it possible to very quickly assume a restful position and also be quick to get up and get going. Most people put up a tent, ground cloth, stakes; it's very time consuming. When you went without anything, naturally you will curl up with your knees against your chest, no wasting any extra warmth; you could use your jacket more often with a fabric addition stitched into the front so you could curl up inside quickly.

matting in the grass. A gradual descent takes you past tiny Heart Lake, full of alpine columbine tucked in the rocks on the trail along its eastern shore. As you approach the two Sallie Keyes Lakes, look out for the little elephant's-heads in the open meadows before the trail splits down the middle of the two lakes. Excellent camping can be found in between the lakes, surrounded by beautiful stands of lodgepoles. From here the trail drops dramatically down a dry and exposed slope to the South Fork of the San Joaquin River along with side trails to MTR and Florence Lake.

A sturdy footbridge over Fish Creek

Silver Pass Creek cascades
right across the JMT

BEST CAMPSITE IN THIS SECTION

LAKE VIRGINIA

Before you make the steep descent into Tully Hole and Fish Creek, it is highly recommended you stop at Lake Virginia. Take time to explore the terrain and open meadows near the shore, which is covered with vivid penstemon and paintbrushes. Smack-dab in the middle of a region where the granite and metavolcanic rocks converge, the views of the surrounding formations can be incredible. The JMT wraps gently around the northeastern edge of the lake, where you can find campsites ranging from thick pine forests and open meadows to right up against the talus fields. Sunrises and sunsets are spectacular and offer some incredible views and reflections off the lake.

SECTION 4

MUIR TRAIL RANCH TO LECONTE CANYON

The Kings Headwaters

Sierra Nevada - Original Purchase Fund from the Mary Reynolds Foundatin, Z. Smith Reynolds Foundation, ARCA, and Anne Cannon Forsyth ALBERT BIERSTADT

Common small mammal on the trail, the Alpine Chipmunk

SECTION 4
MUIR TRAIL RANCH TO LECONTE CANYON

LOCATION: John Muir Wilderness, Sierra National Forest, Kings Canyon National Park, Sequoia and Kings Canyon Wilderness

LENGTH: 26.5 mi.

ELEVATION GAIN/ LOSS (NORTH -> SOUTH): +5,650 ft./ –5,300 ft.

LOWEST POINT: MTR Cutoff Trail South & Florence Lake Trail, 7,900 ft.

HIGHEST POINT: Muir Pass, 11,955 ft.

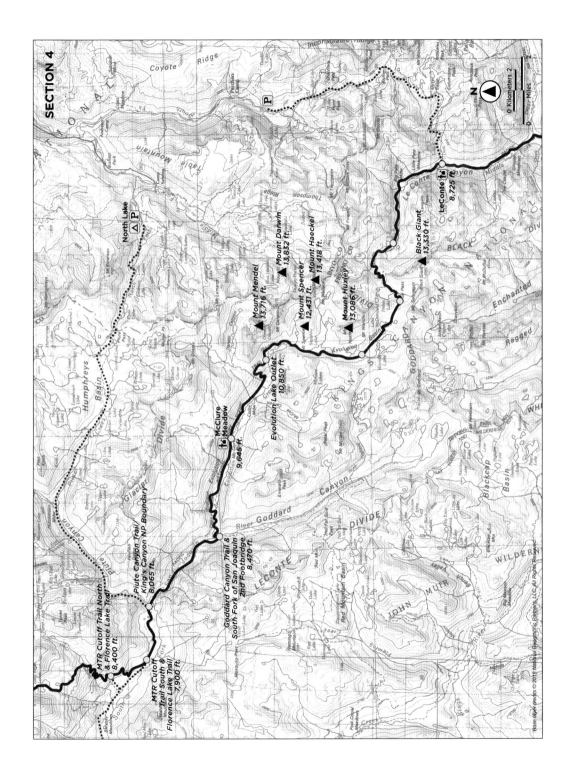

Coyote Ridge

P

North Lake
△ P

Mount Mendel
13,716 ft.

Mount Darwin
13,832 ft.

Mount Spencer
12,431 ft.

Mount Haeckel
13,418 ft.

Mount Huxley
13,086 ft.

Black Giant
13,330 ft.

LeConte
8,725 ft.

Evolution Lake Outlet
10,850 ft.

McClure
Meadow
9,645 ft.

MTR Cutoff Trail North
& Florence Lake Trail
8,400 ft.

Piute Canyon Trail/
King's Canyon NP Boundary
8,065 ft.

MTR Cutoff
Trail South &
Florence Lake Trail
7,900 ft.

Goddard Canyon Trail &
South Fork of San Joaquin
2nd Footbridge
8,470 ft.

Goddard River

N

0 Kilometers 2
0 Miles 2

MILEAGE MARKERS NORTH TO SOUTH

SECTION	TOTAL	ELEVATION	LANDMARK
0	106.2	7,900	MTR Cutoff Trail South & Florence Lake Trail
1.8	108	8,065	Piute Canyon Trail/King's Canyon NP Boundary
5.3	111.5	8,470	Goddard Canyon Trail & South Fork of San Joaquin 2nd Footbridge
9.4	115.6	9,645	McClure Meadow Ranger Station
12.9	119.1	10,850	Evolution Lake Outlet
16.8	123	11,420	Wanda Lake Outlet
18.7	124.9	11,955	Muir Pass
22.6	128.8	10,315	Starr Camp
26.5	132.7	8,725	Bishop Pass Trail/LeConte Ranger Station

*campground with bear boxes

ELEVATION PROFILE

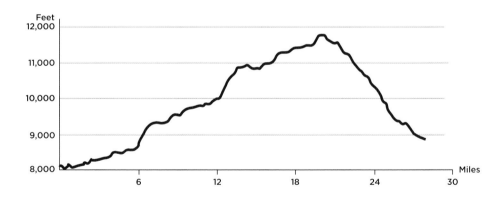

ALTERNATE TRAIL ACCESS POINTS

>> Piute Canyon Trail – 16.5 miles

>> Bishop Pass Trail – 14.1 miles

INTRODUCTION

OVER THE COURSE OF 24 HOURS FROM MUIR PASS TO LECONTE CANYON, I was chased by more lightning and pelted by more rain than on any other trip in the Sierra to date. As I slowly ascended the trail past Lake McDermand up toward John Muir's namesake hut and pass, I noticed the ambient light changing all around me. Black clouds had snuck up and were rolling in behind me to the north; the sunshine ahead on the pass poked fun at me, tempting me to move faster up the steep and rocky alpine terrain. I could see Caymin slowly trekking up the pass still basking in the sunlight and I wanted to be right there with him before I got soaked.

The rain came in short waves, gently sprinkling the exposed dirt and granite blocks dashed across the barren landscape, producing the petrichor, that deep earthy aroma of rain we all know and love. At the top of the pass at 11,955 feet, I took off my

> ## THE CLEAREST WAY INTO THE UNIVERSE IS THROUGH A FOREST WILDERNESS.
> —*John Muir*

pack in the hut to take some photos and enjoy the view. That lasted all of 3 minutes before the first clap of thunder to the north made me jump. I thought *I better get out of here, stat,* as lightning was visible in the distance striking down onto Evolution Basin.

The warm sun was still blanketing the south side of Muir Pass as I hustled down the snowiest terrain on the trail yet, keeping just ahead of the looming storm system. Quickly passing the striking Helen Lake and the headwaters to the Middle Fork of the Kings River, I made my way down toward the unnamed lakes perched just above 10,000 feet to find a protected site for the evening.

A pack llama along the trail

A few miles later I ran back into Caymin at a nice campsite and set my tent up on a small, protected bluff well above the Kings, which seemed like an acceptable location in case a storm came through. Caymin and I enjoyed dinner watching a vivid sunset cast across throngs of cumulonimbus clouds in the distance while a cascading waterfall played a lovely melody just below.

Crack! I'm up! My eyes are pie-size and staring at the

Evolution Creek cascades into a
warm sunset down valley

ceiling of my tent. It's 3 a.m. and I hear nothing now, then the universe rumbles intensely right into the ground, making way for another *crack!* It was at that moment the heavens unzipped and a deluge of biblical proportions came forth, turning my tent into Noah's Arc. The parched earth couldn't absorb the rain fast enough and I could see a river of rainwater flowing effortlessly between my ground cloth and tent. I had to act quickly if I wanted to avoid being completely drenched. I grabbed my waterproof Mountain Hardwear pack from the vestibule and shoved every other loose item into it for protection. This went at the bottom of my sleeping pad, and I shoved my feet into the top of the pack so myself and all my items were on this little inflatable sleeping "raft," protected from the surprise river I was caught on top of. Caymin, who was also in the heart of the storm, wrote in his journal "The lightning and thunder turned downright terrifying as two or three of the strikes were followed by ear splitting thunder only a split second later and made the ground feel as though it was shaking and being split in half beneath me. It rained so hard during that second go around that the drops hitting the ground were splashing up inside of my rainfly near the foot of my tent and creating some small puddles at the bottom."

There was no sleep for the next 2 hours; all I could do was count the seconds between thunder and lightning, hoping it was passing through. But it didn't. The storm circled above, tossing bolts of electricity within a mere quarter mile of my tent while earth-shattering thunder fulminated about. I was reminded of a line from *The Mountains of California by* John Muir: "Zigzag lances of lightning followed each other in quick succession, and the thunder was so gloriously loud and massive it seemed as if surely an entire mountain was being shattered at every stroke."

Peter Croft among the Evolution Range
GALEN ROWELL

Lemmon's Indian paintbrush

Rock fringe

Pennyroyal a.k.a. coyote mint

Sneezeweed

White mountain heather

Sticky cinquefoil

Quaint camping along
the South Fork of the
San Joaquin River

Clark's Nutcracker

By 5 a.m. no mountains had shattered on top of my head—the storm decided it was through with its torment for the moment and moved on. I drifted listlessly in and out of sleep until 8 a.m., when I awoke to gray skies, made some coffee, and assessed the damage. Nearly every swatch of my gear was wet in some form. I was going to have to pack everything soaking and wait for the sun to hopefully come out later in the day. No sooner had I finished my coffee than I noticed menacing clouds inching in from the south, blotting out the vast LeConte Canyon. Gear was heaved into my pack haplessly, my raincoat went on, and as soon as I finished lacing my shoes, the downpour commenced, trailed by the guttural rumble of ensuing thunder.

I was chased down steep granite switchbacks by the storm, my footing never more sure as I envisioned six steps ahead at all times. Hiking poles became third and fourth legs as I vaulted over small creeks and plunged off massive blocks along the trail. I covered over 7 miles in just under 2 hours, drawn by the ever-present patch of sunlight I could see far below. My rapid pace got me to the Palisade Creek junction, where I took off my wet clothes and gear to let the sun get to work. It felt as if I had escaped the ninth circle of the Inferno and was reborn into Paradiso as I looked back up to where

Looking south toward the black
mass of the Goddard Divide

Muir Pass would have been if it weren't for the murky clouds disfiguring the entire skyline to the north. I was reminded of Dante's words "The path to paradise begins in hell" as I thought ahead to the Palisade Basin, my personal paradise.

OVERVIEW

From the trail junctions with Florence Lake and MTR, you trek south toward Kings Canyon National Park through Jeffrey pines and western junipers. The trail parallels the San Joaquin as it surges through dark-colored metamorphic rock. You soon arrive at a footbridge across Piute Creek, where you will find a long side trail that will lead to the North Lake trailhead and access to the town of Bishop. Just beyond this footbridge, you cross the boundary into Kings Canyon, with many fine campsites along the river.

Continuing along the San Joaquin, the trail meanders in and out of stands of lodgepole pine with great views of Pavilion Dome to the north. You will cross the San Joaquin twice within a mile on sturdy footbridges. The second crossing offers excellent camping and marks the start of the steep ascent into Evolution Valley. Leaving the San Joaquin behind, you will now follow Evolution Creek as it cascades down

High atop Muir Pass, the Muir Hut weathers
the night under the Milky Way
DARK SKY PHOTOGRAPHY

metamorphic rock. The trail switchbacks up steep terrain, leading you to a major river crossing that in wet years has an alternate option a short way up the creek in Evolution Meadow. As the trail mellows out in the meadow, you'll notice wildflowers like paintbrushes, lupines, and sneezeweed start to reappear.

The farther down the valley you continue, the better the view becomes of the magnificent skyline of the Evolution Range. You will be fully entertained with the incredible amount of wildlife at play in the meadows, including mallards and mule deer, and the creek that's bursting with brook trout. You have one steep ascent left before entering Evolution Basin perched above. The trail switchbacks through granite features and slabs as the trees begin to become more stunted, giving way to the alpine terrain.

Evolution Basin's impressive skyline of peaks were named by trail pioneer Theodore Solomons on an explorative expedition in 1895. Just over a century later that same skyline was first climbed in one push by Sierra mountaineering legend Peter Croft in a day. As you enter the basin on the northern

RESUPPLY LOCATIONS

Bishop Post Office
Phone: (760) 873-3526
Mail packages to:

(Your Name)
c/o General Delivery
Bishop Post Office
585 West Line St.
Bishop, CA 93514
Arriving by: ETA

NEVER BEFORE HAD I SEEN SO GLORIOUS A LANDSCAPE, AS BOUNDLESS AN AFFLUENCE OF SUBLIME MOUNTAIN BEAUTY. THE MOST EXTRAVAGANT DESCRIPTION I MIGHT GIVE OF THIS VIEW TO ANY ONE WHO HAD NOT SEEN SIMILAR LANDSCAPES WITH HIS OWN EYES WOULD NOT SO MUCH AS HINT ITS GRANDEUR AND THE SPIRITUAL GLOW THAT COVERED IT.

—*John Muir*

edge of Evolution Lake, you are treated with sweeping views of the entire range, possibly instilling dreams of greatness like these two visionaries preceding us. It is highly recommended you take your time walking up Evolution Basin, an ever-changing landscape steeped in geologic history. You can find many fine campsites along any one of the alpine lakes leading up to Muir Pass. As you follow water sources up from the main basin, multitudes of wildflowers will be found along the edges of the trail peeking out of rocks and near small seeps of water. Among them are pennyroyal, white mountain heather, and rock fringe.

Directly to your south lies the dark metamorphic mass of Mt. Goddard and the Goddard Divide, likely the source of all the metamorphic rock found along the trail leading up to Evolution Basin. As you gradually ascend toward Wanda Lake, named after John Muir's oldest daughter, you will pass beautiful slabs where the lake's outlet flows down into Evolution Lake; you can find small campsites along the shores of all the lakes. From here you get your first view of Muir Pass and Muir Hut dwarfed by the tremendous Black Giant perched just to its east. This wide-open alpine terrain is much different from the tight Evolution Basin you just came from. The historical octagonal

Geology Notes from Michael Hassan

Along with some of the most awesome glacial topography the John Muir Trail has to offer, Evolution Valley provides a glimpse of topography formed by a more contemporary geologic process. At the northern portion of Evolution Lake, the trail runs on top of several features called alluvial fans. Recognizable as wedges protruding from several small valleys that enter Evolution Valley, these fan-shaped piles of nonvegetated debris are formed as flows of water move pieces of rock downhill and out of the mountains. During periods of heavy precipitation, enormous amounts of rock can accumulate at the base of these fans, dramatically changing the landscape in very short time periods.

PHOTOGRAPHY TIP:
DIGITAL CAMERAS IN THE BACKCOUNTRY

The world of photography has made a huge transition from film cameras to digital, and it has opened up photography as a hobby for many aspiring photographers. When backpacking with your digital camera, you may need some extra gear and precautions to make the experience all the more enjoyable and ensure you take great photos to share with your friends and family.

Having a cleaning cloth and UV filter will help keep your lens clean and protected in the field. When changing lenses, find an area with little or no wind, or use a jacket to shield the camera, as this will prevent dust particles from getting onto your sensor or mirror. Make sure to have a sturdy case for your camera with a way to attach it to you or your pack for easy access, allowing you to take pictures quicker and easier. Backup batteries for your camera are essential on an extended trip; you may also consider a solar charger to charge as you go. Lastly, temperatures at night can drop below freezing even during the summer months. If it's cold, take all your batteries out and sleep with them in your pocket or at the bottom of your sleeping bag. This will help preserve the battery life so when morning comes you can snap that amazing sunrise!

Approaching
LeConte Canyon

A stormy sunset full of color

EXCERPTS FROM THE BACKCOUNTRY

Peter Croft – Avid Sierra Climber and Adventurer, SMG
Guide, Underhill Award Winner, Author, Speaker

My first time on the Evolution Traverse with Galen Rowell gave me a handful of etched moments that I'll never forget. Perhaps the one that summed up the experience was as I approached camp at the tail end of the day. Galen had ditched out on the traverse roughly halfway through, and so I'd finished the last three or four peaks on my own. After descending to the JMT, I took a shortcut around the west side of Evolution Lake to reach our base camp at the far end. As I took off my shoes and waded the shallows, a shocking sunset took hold and cast a peach-pink alpenglow the length of the mountains I'd just traversed. The others didn't see me coming and I could see Galen, Barbara, and a handful of friends milling around with after-dinner drinks in hand—toasting the life, I suppose. I stood there for a bit, feeling the cold water on bruised feet, looking down at the green marshy lakeside and up at the fiery skyline—and then across at my friends laughing and celebrating. It was a crystalline moment that summed up the best of living in this world.

Andrew Turchon – AT & JMT Thru-Hiker, Educator

I hiked through what felt like an intractable winter, more like a mountaineering endurance event than a long-distance hike. Completing the JMT in 2011 demanded that I trudge through soupy, knee-high snow around Sunrise Mountain, glissade down the backside of Pinchot Pass, cross the icy chest-high San Joaquin River, tiptoe over sketchy snow bridges, and skirt miles of glaciated valleys covered by snow disks. Outside of summiting Mt. Whitney, my most memorable experience was a night hike through Evolution Basin. The trail appeared as a thin white ribbon threading itself through ice-covered lakes backlit by the glow of the moon and the light of my headlamp. My JMT experience was ultimately shaped by an extended winter that fundamentally changed the trail's character. Even still, I would do it all again, but next time I hope to see more of the trail along the way.

hut on the summit was built in 1930 by the Sierra Club and offers an emergency shelter for hikers and rangers; many people have been protected here in dire situations.

Descending in a northeastern direction down Muir Pass will typically bring you across some of the larger snow patches on the trail, all while views of the vibrant blue waters of Helen Lake, named after John Muir's youngest daughter, expand in front of you and lead to the craggy headwaters of the Kings River. Many wildflowers will once again appear along the sides of the trail as you descend, like the gigantic patch of mountaineer shooting stars on the south shore of the unnamed lake. The trail makes a sharp drop down toward the stunted whitebark pines, passing a handful of unnamed lakes as you follow the Kings River. Many fine campsites can be found on both sides of the river, particularly Starr

> WHEN WE TRY TO PICK OUT ANYTHING BY ITSELF, WE FIND IT HITCHED TO EVERYTHING ELSE IN THE UNIVERSE.
>
> —*John Muir*

Camp around the 10,300-foot mark, with superb views down to LeConte Canyon.

Steep switchbacks down a blasted cliff continue to follow the turbulent and often cascading Kings River. Soon wide-open views of LeConte Canyon appear to your south and are fringed by Langille Peak, Giraud Peak, the Citadel, and the Devils Crags. As you pass many excellent camping opportunities in Big and Little Pete Meadows, the descent subsides a bit and the Kings River starts to snake through LeConte in a lazy manner. Soon you arrive at the LeConte Ranger Station, where you can find the junction to the Bishop Pass Trail, a popular route to access the town of Bishop.

BEST CAMPSITES IN THIS SECTION

EVOLUTION LAKE

The strong draw toward the Evolution Basin can be felt as soon as you leave the Muir Trail Ranch and begin to weave your way into Kings Canyon National Park along the San Joaquin River. From McClure Meadow the whole range is on display and beckons you to keep walking those last few miles, where you will be rewarded with epic camping options. Beautiful granite slabs line the northern end of the lake and can frequently be occupied by other campers if you don't arrive early enough. If that's the case, follow a side trail to the lake outlet and look for some nice flat sites along the water. You can also continue across the creek to find some more seclusion. The sun sets right down Evolution Valley in the summer and blankets the mountain range in a perfect cover of oranges and pinks.

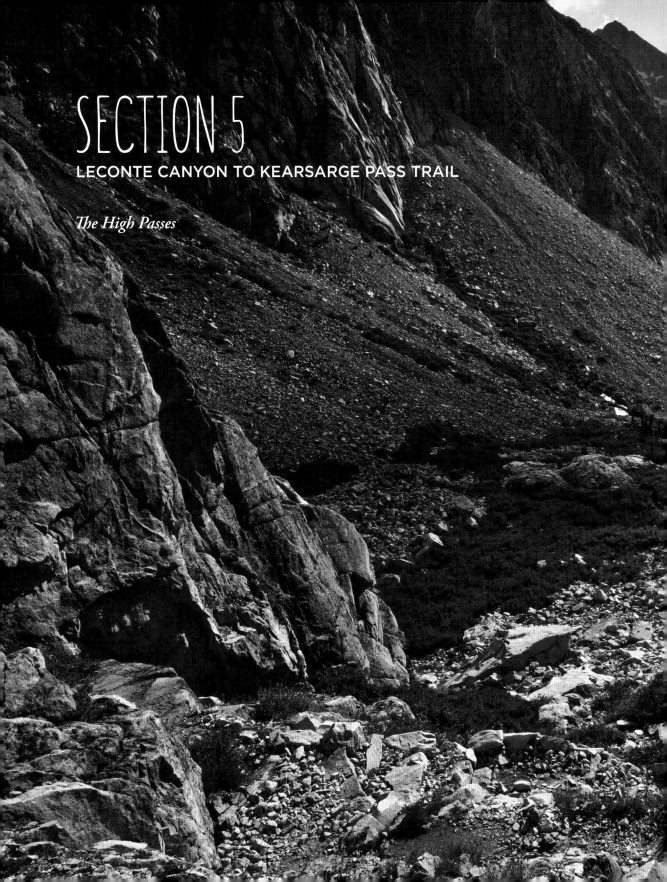

SECTION 5
LECONTE CANYON TO KEARSARGE PASS TRAIL

The High Passes

Looking back toward the Devils Crags from the Golden Staircase

Dusk over the
Palisades
VERN CLEVENGER

SECTION 5
LECONTE CANYON TO KEARSARGE PASS TRAIL

LOCATION: Kings Canyon National Park, Sequoia and Kings Canyon Wilderness

LENGTH: 43.0 miles

ELEVATION GAIN/ LOSS (NORTH -> SOUTH): +11,220 ft./ –9,235 ft.

LOWEST POINT: Palisade Creek & Middle Fork Trail, 8,025 ft.

HIGHEST POINT: Pinchot Pass, 12,090 ft.

GOING TO THE MOUNTAINS
IS GOING HOME.
—*John Muir*

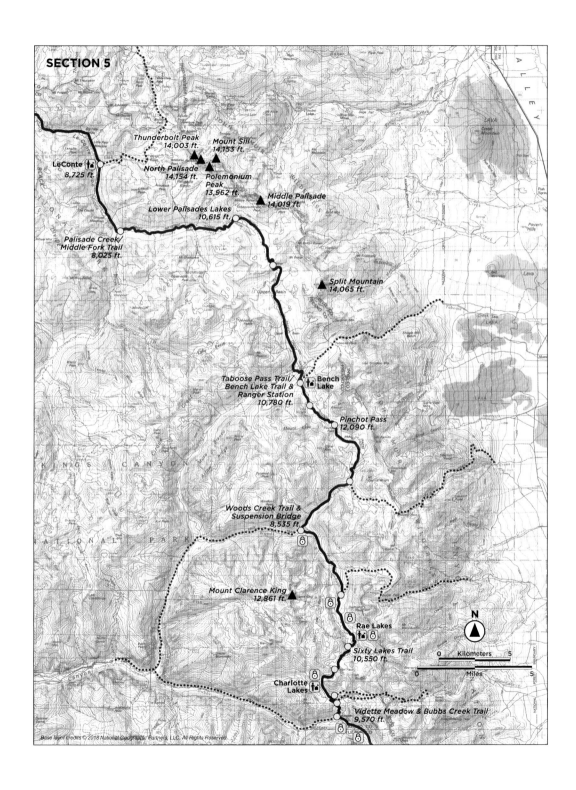

Thunderbolt Peak
14,003 ft.

Mount Sill
14,153 ft.

LeConte
8,725 ft.

North Palisade
14,154 ft.

Polemonium
Peak
13,962 ft.

Middle Palisade
14,019 ft.

Lower Palisades Lakes
10,615 ft.

Palisade Creek/
Middle Fork Trail
8,025 ft.

Split Mountain
14,065 ft.

Taboose Pass Trail/
Bench Lake Trail &
Ranger Station
10,780 ft.

Bench
Lake

Pinchot Pass
12,090 ft.

Woods Creek Trail &
Suspension Bridge
8,535 ft.

Mount Clarence King
12,861 ft.

Rae Lakes

Sixty Lakes Trail
10,550 ft.

Charlotte
Lakes

Vidette Meadow & Bubbs Creek Trail
9,570 ft.

KINGS CANYON

NATIONAL PARK

N

Kilometers   5

Miles

5

MILEAGE MARKERS NORTH TO SOUTH

SECTION	TOTAL	ELEVATION	LANDMARK
0	132.7	8,725	Bishop Pass Trail/LeConte Ranger Station
3.4	136.1	8,025	Palisade Creek/Middle Fork Trail
10.1	142.8	10,615	Lower Palisades Lakes
14	146.7	12,085	Mather Pass
20.8	153.5	10,780	Taboose Pass Trail/Bench Lake Trail & Ranger Station
22.3	155	11,120	Lake Marjorie
23.8	156.5	12,090	Pinchot Pass
27.6	160.3	10,355	Sawmill Pass Trail
31.4	164.1	8,535	Woods Creek Trail & Suspension Bridge*
35.5	168.2	10,230	Dollar Lake & Baxter Pass Trail
38.5	171.2	10,550	Sixty Lakes Trail
40.3	173	11,975	Glen Pass
42.4	175.1	10,790	Kearsarge Pass Trail & Charlotte Lake Ranger Station*
43	175.7	10,525	Bullfrog Lake Trail to Kearsarge Pass

*campground with bear boxes

ELEVATION PROFILE

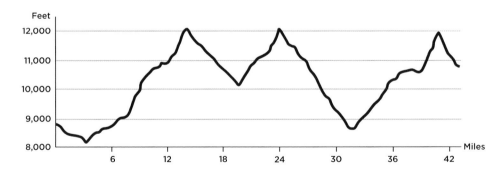

CLIMB THE MOUNTAINS AND GET THEIR GOOD TIDINGS.

—John Muir

INTRODUCTION

IN 1996, AT THE PLIABLE AGE OF 16, I flew out to California for my second Sierra backpacking trip in as many years. This time I felt more confident about the journey. I knew what to expect out of the Sierra; the weather, the terrain, and all of the hazards that came along with it. This left me more focused to observe the grandiose scenery I would be surrounded by for the next week.

My uncle and I chose to hike up into the dramatic Palisade group. We slowly followed the enchainment of lakes along the North Fork of Big Pine Creek on the way to our final unspoiled campsite at Third Lake. I had appropriately brought along a collection of essays from John Muir. There honestly could've been no better place to dive into the words crafted by this incredible naturalist. As the mighty peaks of the 14,000-foot-high Palisade Crest watched over us day and night, Muir's words resonated in my mind, setting the tone for a true adventure: "In every walk with nature one receives far more than he seeks."

On our fourth day we decided to take a hike up to the Palisade Glacier and the base of North Palisade, a peak Norman Clyde described as "one of the most striking peaks in the Sierra Nevada." As we scrambled along car-size blocks of granite to the west of Temple Crag and Mt. Gayley, the view continued to increase dramatically. An hour of physical hiking and climbing brought us up to a ridge perched above the most electric-neon-blue lake my eyes have ever seen, laden with fresh chunks of ice gently floating around with no foreseeable destination. I was reminded of Clyde's words again: "The magnificent Palisades, whose dark serrated forms rise above a series of glaciers that cling to their bases and send icy fingers far up the steep chutes that furrow their northern fronts."

I had never experienced such raw beauty in nature until this moment. Staring at those high granite summits above me, their icy couloirs and the bevy of glacial tarns cast around the landscape, I knew right then and there that these mountains were going to be in my heart and soul, playing a major role in my life from this point forward.

Over the next twenty years, I would hone my skills backpacking thousands of miles and rock climbing hundreds of routes across the country, all while keeping the Sierra

ALTERNATE TRAIL ACCESS POINTS

>> Taboose Pass Trail – 9.4 miles

>> Sawmill Pass Trail – 13.5 miles

>> Woods Creek Trail – 15.2 miles

>> Baxter Pass Trail – 10.6 miles

>> Kearsarge Pass Trail – 7.0 miles

>> Bullfrog Lake Trail – 7.0 miles

Arrow Peak reflected on
Bench Lake at sunrise

Nevada close to my heart. Now, here I was as a 37-year-old, en route to the region that planted the inspiration over two decades ago to live a life dedicated to the outdoors. This time I was hiking in on the southern side of the Palisade Crest, prepared to stare at summits I've climbed in years past.

For me the Palisade Basin was one of the locations I most looked forward to visiting while hiking the John Muir Trail. I had just escaped one of the most dramatic lightning storms I'd ever experienced, and as the sun warmed the earth, I felt a special buzz circulating through my body. I cast off toward the Golden Staircase just as the sun was low enough to bring out the namesake colors along this notoriously steep section. Every turn brought a new scent emanating from the patches of varying wildflowers waving at me as the wind fanned their stems and petals in unison. I marched forward higher and higher into the alpine zone.

Twenty years ago I couldn't help but laugh when I first laid my eyes on that neon-blue lake and the shark-tooth peaks above. It just didn't look real—there's no way things like this exist in a world I can be a part of. But that's the thing: The Range of Light surprises even the most veteran of explorers day in and day out. As I crested that last switchback on the Golden Staircase, I got my first unbroken view of the entire Palisade Crest and I just had to stop, drop my pack, and have a good laugh. This is real and it is just as extraordinary as it was the first time.

Alpine goldenrod

Fleabane daisy

Kelly's tiger lily

Sierra primrose

Shrubby cinquefoil

Western eupatorium

OVERVIEW

As the trail descends from the Bishop Pass trail junction, you will pass many camping opportunities along the gentle Middle Fork of the Kings River under stands of lodgepoles. LeConte Canyon culminates at the Palisade Creek and Middle Fork junction—from here your official journey to the Golden Staircase and Palisade Basin begins. A long and gentle approach brings you through Deer Meadow, full of ample camping options for those who want to tackle the next section with fresh legs in the morning. The Golden Staircase sends you quickly up 1,600 feet of beaming granite switchbacks. It's hard to imagine the amount of work that went into discovering a path, mapping it out, and then creating it. Hundreds of man-hours are to thank for giving us access to one of the most pristine alpine regions in California. The views west of the Devils Crags and Citadel increase dramatically as you rise higher through

> THESE FLEETING SKY MOUNTAINS ARE AS SUBSTANTIAL AND SIGNIFICANT AS THE MORE LASTING UPHEAVALS OF GRANITE BENEATH THEM. BOTH ALIKE ARE BUILT UP AND DIE, AND IN GOD'S CALENDAR DIFFERENCE OF DURATION IS NOTHING.
>
> —*John Muir*

Ascending Mather Pass with the Palisade basin to the north

Wood's Creek tumbles down towards the Castle Domes

patches of wildflowers at every turn. You can easily spot crimson columbines and Kelly's tiger lilies near the streamlets and pink western eupatorium along the dry stretches.

As you reach the apex of the Golden Staircase, a jaw-dropping view awaits of the Palisade Crest, including Norman Clyde Peak, Middle Palisade, and Disappointment

Geology Notes from Michael Hassan

Just north of Mather Pass, the JMT passes near the Palisade Glacier, the largest glacier in the Sierra. Palisade Glacier reached its maximum size during a period of minor cooling 170 to 250 years ago, and has since been melting and retreating uphill. Early in the glacier's recession, the rocks suspended in the ice at the lowest regions of the glacier were deposited in a large pile called a moraine. One of the special features of this glacier is that this moraine acts as a dam for meltwater coming off the glacier, forming a milky, turquoise, proglacial lake downstream of the toe (lowest point) of the glacier.

PHOTOGRAPHY TIP: CLAUDE FIDDLER, 📷 DEDICATION TO THE IMAGE

The Kings River canyons are steep, avalanche scoured clefts sliced into the heart of the High Sierra. The side creeks draining into the canyons are turbulent, roaring, and beautiful. I was at the top of one of these creeks across from the Devils Crags when I made this picture in August of 1988. For me these were the days of 4x5 view camera on tripod. The 4x5 was the only camera I used or

The Devils Crags from below Observation Peak
CLAUDE FIDDLER

owned. I worked with only one lens. A 150-millimeter APO Rodenstock carried a Pentax Spotmeter, three film holders, and I changed film in my sleeping bag at night. When I made this picture I used Kodak VPL negative sheet film. The film had very low contrast, terrible color cross over, and tolerated long exposures. A necessity when shooting at tight F stops. I could have used a 35 mm camera or a medium format camera and film but I wanted the highest image quality available at the time. My gear was trimmed to a bare minimum. My wife Nancy and I would be out in the backcountry on week- to month-long trips and it seems crazy that I'd carry heavy and bulky camera gear but I really cared about my pictures. I was also thoroughly obsessed with climbing backcountry granite walls, so add in a rope and climbing gear and I was usually carrying seventy to eighty pounds on our trips.

When I walked into this scene I was floored by the drama. Nancy and I set up camp and I walked out on granite slabs above the lake to see if I could set my tripod where I needed to. I probably sat for three hours watching the light change. I only had six sheets of film to expose. As the sun set I waited for optimal lighting and made three exposures.

It has taken me decades to realize a print that does justice to the scene.

Peak. Stop and enjoy the view along the creek in the narrow canyon just below Palisade Lake. The interesting rock formations are ringed by wildflowers like the bright mountain pride penstemon. Palisade Lake offers a variety of camping opportunities on either shore; if it is too crowded, continue down the trail, where more sites can be found at Upper Palisade Lake.

As the trail turns to pure rock, the incline escalates and affords you greater views north of the Palisade Range. More 14,000-foot peaks, like North Palisade and Mt. Sill, come into sight. You can fully appreciate the view in all directions atop the 12,085-foot summit of Mather Pass, where another 14,000-foot peak, Split Mountain, stands out to the southeast. Sandy trail leads quickly down into Upper Basin and descends south along the headwaters of the South Fork of the Kings River. You will find ample camping opportunities both above the tree line and as you enter the first stands of lodgepole pines below.

In most seasons hikers face two river crossings with no bridges available. The South Fork of the Kings and another creek at the trail junctions to Bench Lake and Taboose Pass both can be tricky in early season. The Bench Lake Ranger Station can also be found a short distance off the trail here; in 1996 it was the site of a massive search-and-rescue effort for a mysteriously missing ranger, Randy Morgenson, a 28-year veteran of the backcountry. Check out the enigmatic book *The Last Season* by Eric Blehm. If it

RESUPPLY LOCATIONS

Big Pine Post Office
Phone: (760) 938-2542
Mail packages to:

(Your Name)
c/o General Delivery
Big Pine Post Office
140 North Main St.
Big Pine, CA 93513
Arriving by: ETA

Independence Post Office
Phone: (760) 878-2210
Mail packages to:

(Your Name)
c/o General Delivery
Independence Post Office
101 South Edwards St.
Independence, CA 93526
Arriving by: ETA

Mount Williamson Motel
Hiker Resupply and Lodging
Contact Strider at (760) 878-2121
Email: MtWilliamsonMotel@gmail.com
Mail packages to:

(Your name)
Mt. Williamson Motel and Base Camp
PO Box 128
Independence, CA 93526
Arriving by: ETA

Descending through talus and Foxtail Pines to Charlotte Lake

Sunset, Charlotte Dome, and granite reflections

fits your schedule, a hike out to Bench Lake is well worth it, overlooking the western slope of the Sierra and crowned off by the perfectly triangular Arrow Peak.

The trail now ascends past a handful of unnamed tarns, sporting excellent camping options, on the way to the deep blue shores of Lake Marjorie. As the trail now steepens toward Pinchot Pass, glacial lakes appear in progressively brighter shades of neon blue the higher you climb. From atop the 12,090-foot Pinchot Pass, you can see north to the Palisade range and south toward the giant red metamorphic Crater Mountain and Woods Creek drainage.

EXCERPTS FROM THE BACKCOUNTRY

Darin McQuoid – Expedition Kayaker, Photographer, darinmcquoid.com

The Middle Fork of the Kings River from LeConte Canyon to Yucca Point is considered the pinnacle of expedition kayaking in the United States. Everything about the run is epic. It has an 8-hour one-way shuttle, a 14-mile hike over 12,000-foot Bishop Pass and 40 miles of world-class whitewater, dropping 7,000 vertical feet. We bring almost a hundred pounds of gear between the kayak, paddling gear, and food needed to paddle for four days down the Middle Kings. If these trails didn't exist, there is no way we could access the rivers for kayaking.

Once on the Middle Kings, only a short bit of mank has to be endured before the river starts to turn into every expedition kayaker's dream: big drops in gorgeous scenery. Take away the length, wilderness setting, and scenery of the Middle Kings and it would still be an awesome river just for the amount of quality whitewater it contains. The Bottom Nine has a reputation for dishing out trouble to tired kayakers. It's filled with big boulder gardens full of hungry holes and the occasional portage, all nonstop for 9 miles. There is nowhere else in the world where such a high quality of whitewater is combined with perfect weather and long, remote sections that take days to journey down yet have great access at the start and finish.

Gwendolyn Ostrosky – Long-Distance Trail Runner (Rae Lakes Loop—42 Miles in 13 Hours), Outdoor Enthusiast

Part of what I love about trail running in the Sierra Nevada is the ability to see so much in such a short period of time. There are endless places to go and see; there is never an end to the bucket list. The beauty of traveling light and running a long route is the ability to traverse somewhat boring sections quickly while still slowing down to enjoy the prettier sections. It's definitely important to slow down sometimes to notice and appreciate the little things, like sunlight through tree branches, or the sounds of nature unaccompanied by heavy breathing and clothing rustling. Balancing speed and distance is key!

Kayaking the Middle
Fork of the Kings River
signature Money Drop
DARIN MCQUOID

A tributary to the South
Fork of the Kings River

On the right, the summit of Mount Brewer catches first sun

Beautiful open terrain brings you gradually past a series of lakes and tarns that have been known to host mountain yellow-legged frogs and their tadpoles. You continue to descend past foxtail pines and western junipers as the trail follows Woods Creek tumbling down granite slabs on the way to the famous "Golden Gate of the Sierra," the Woods Creek Suspension Bridge. From the bridge you hike through dense forest of lodgepole and Jeffrey pines, cross a wide section of the South Fork of Woods Creek, and pass a variety of glacial moraines as you ascend toward the Rae Lakes Basin.

The first lake you arrive at is the petite Dollar Lake, with stupendous reflections of Fin Dome to the south and limited camping options. Mellow terrain takes you through marshy meadows on the way to Arrowhead Lake, then Rae Lakes, where you can find campsites with food-storage lockers and a seasonal ranger station. At the southern end of Rae Lakes, you begin the steep ascent up rocky Glen Pass with views to the east of the colorful Painted Lady. The talus and steep cliffs around Glen Pass are a prime location for bighorn sheep, and if you don't happen to see one, the views of the half dozen glacial tarns tucked into the base of the pass are sure to please the eyes.

The windy summit of Glen Pass has dizzying views south into a narrow canyon with a handful of glacial tarns tucked away. Past these a steep descent takes you past stately foxtail pines and to Charlotte Lake, where just to the west lies the prominent Charlotte Dome, hosting what Sierra climbing expert R. J. Secor calls "one of the world's finest rock climbs." The 1,500-foot-long South Face, first ascended

Mount Jordan, Table Mountain, and
Thunder Mountain at sunset

Fin Dome evening reflection off Dollar Lake

by climbing legends Fred Becky and Galen Rowell in 1970, climbs the southern profile of the dome and typically takes a full day to ascend. As the trail finishes its descent, you reach junctions to Charlotte Lake and Kearsarge Pass. The latter takes you to Onion Valley trailhead with access to the town of Independence, the last major resupply option on the trail.

An evening storm approaches Glen Pass

BEST CAMPSITE IN THIS SECTION

RAE LAKES BASIN

Instead of trying to narrow this section into one awesome campsite, it is best to consider the entire Rae Lakes Basin when choosing a site. From the tiny and slightly weather-protected Dollar Lake with its gorgeous reflections of Fin Dome at the far north end of the basin, to the much larger Rae Lake at the southern end with its incredible alpine feel, surrounded by multiple 12,000- and 13,000-foot peaks, any one of these sites delivers incredible views morning, day, and night. And they provide easy access to multiple side trails straight out of the Sierra. This area sees lots of traffic on the weekends due to the amount of options to access the lakes.

SECTION 6
KEARSARGE PASS TRAIL TO MT. WHITNEY

Over the Divide to Whitney

Remnants of a
thunderstorm on
Mount Whitney

Looking north into the Bubb's Creek drainage dominated by University Peak

SECTION 6
KEARSARGE PASS TRAIL TO MT. WHITNEY

LOCATION: Kings Canyon National Park, Sequoia National Park, Sequoia and Kings Canyon Wilderness, Inyo National Forest

LENGTH: 29.5 mi.

ELEVATION GAIN/ LOSS (NORTH -> SOUTH): +10,420 ft./ –6,715 ft.

LOWEST POINT: Vidette Meadow and Bubbs Creek Trail, 9,570 ft.

HIGHEST POINT: Mt. Whitney, 14,505 ft.

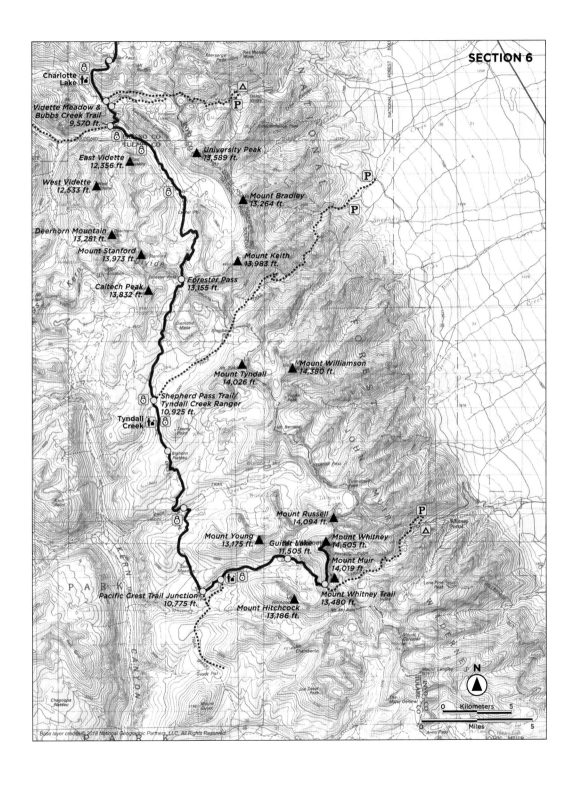

Charlotte Lake

Vidette Meadow & Bubbs Creek Trail
9,570 ft.

East Vidette
12,356 ft.

West Vidette
12,533 ft.

University Peak
13,589 ft.

Mount Bradley
13,264 ft.

Deerhorn Mountain
13,281 ft.

Mount Stanford
13,973 ft

Mount Keith
13,983 ft.

Caltech Peak
13,832 ft.

Forester Pass
13,155 ft.

Mount Williamson
14,380 ft.

Mount Tyndall
14,026 ft.

Shepherd Pass Trail/
Tyndall Creek Ranger
10,925 ft.

Tyndall Creek

Mount Russell
14,094 ft.

Mount Young
13,175 ft.

Guitar Lake
11,505 ft.

Mount Whitney
14,505 ft.

Mount Muir
14,019 ft.

Pacific Crest Trail Junction
10,775 ft.

Mount Hitchcock
13,186 ft.

Mount Whitney Trail
13,480 ft.

N

Kilometers

Miles

MILEAGE MARKERS NORTH TO SOUTH

SECTION	TOTAL	ELEVATION	LANDMARK
0	175.7	10,525	Bullfrog Lake Trail to Kearsarge Pass
1.1	176.8	9,570	Vidette Meadow & Bubbs Creek Trail
8.9	184.6	13,155	Forester Pass
13.4	189.1	10,925	Shepherd Pass Trail*/Tyndall Creek Ranger
15.2	190.9	11,420	Bighorn Plateau
17.8	193.5	10,405	High Sierra Trail Junction/Wallace Creek*
21.2	196.9	10,775	Pacific Crest Trail Junction
22	197.7	10,700	Crabtree Meadow Junction and Ranger Station*
24.7	200.4	11,505	Guitar Lake
27.6	203.3	13,480	Mt. Whitney Trail
29.5	205.2	14,505	Mt. Whitney Summit

*campground with bear boxes

ELEVATION PROFILE

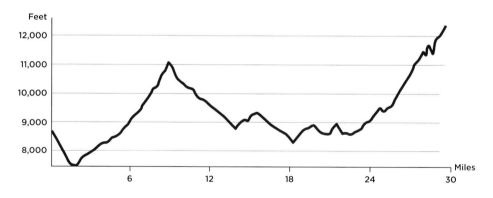

ALTERNATE TRAIL ACCESS POINTS

>> Bubbs Creek Trail – 12.5 miles

>> Shepherd Pass Trail – 13.9 miles

>> PCT South to Cottonwood Pass & Horseshoe Meadow – 20.1 miles

>> Mt. Whitney Trail Crest to Whitney Portal – 8.8 miles

INTRODUCTION

ONE OF THE MOST CRUCIAL ASPECTS TO ANY LONG-DISTANCE TRIP is not only having backpacking skills and being in good physical condition, it's having the support from your family at home and camaraderie with new friends on the trail. I learned the importance of this on the Appalachian Trail: My mother supported me from home by sending resupply packages when I needed them and keeping the excitement alive every time I called from a payphone. I also cherished the many unique friends I made along the way. The

I ONLY WENT OUT FOR A WALK, AND FINALLY CONCLUDED TO STAY OUT TILL SUNDOWN, FOR GOING OUT, I FOUND, WAS REALLY GOING IN.
—*John Muir*

bond we all shared was common, to continue moving north through some of the East Coast's most majestic landscapes toward Mt. Katahdin.

It was no different on the JMT. My supportive and adventurous wife joined me for 6 days from Tuolumne to Red's Meadow. It was the best week on the trail; having her by my side so we could support each other through the obstacles the trail inevitably throws at us was incredible. When my wife had to leave to go back to work, it was a sad day for both of us. But I was able to continue forming friendships with fellow

Amazing trail construction on the south side of Forester Pass

Alpenglow along the Kearsarge
Pinnacles and Mount Rixford

The Kaweah Range

hikers along the way to find that extra support I needed to finish this amazing journey and inspire new ones.

After picking a perfect site below Forester Pass with beautiful views to University Peak and the Kearsarge Pinnacles, a location my family and I have spent a considerable amount of time exploring, I was greeted by my neighbors Steve and Steve, the 60-something-year-olds out on a 10-day excursion. We chatted all evening and over breakfast the next morning, discovering our common love for Washington State University's Cougar Gold white cheddar cheese! It was refreshing to see such youthful spirit in these aging gentlemen; it gave me inspiration to continue following my outdoor pursuits well into the future no matter my age.

That next day as I meandered up the stark terrain of Forester Pass, I could see a pair of hikers mingling at the summit and looked forward to meeting them. Upon my arrival, I was greeted with high fives from PCT thru-hikers Kramers and Red's Cross for summiting the highest pass on the trail yet. As I enjoyed the view to the south, it was as if a divine being from the heavens dipped its chalice into the lakes of purity when Kramers offered me a sip of his freshly opened Cheerwine, a cherry-flavored cola he carried 78 miles from Kennedy Meadows. That sip replenished my fire and put a hop in my step, aiding the swift descent down Forester away from the oncoming black clouds and thunder to the north.

Along the descent to Tyndall Creek

Felwort

Oval-leaved buckwheat

Mountain sorrel

Sky pilot

Shooting star

Yarrow

Alpine meadow and creek
below Forester Pass

Two days later, after being awoken by a multi-ton rockfall that flung giant sparks off the west face of Mt. Whitney, I was relieved to see another hiker as I left camp in the morning. I met Anik at the Guitar Lake inlet—she had just begun her north-bound thru-hike and was heading up to the summit as well. We passed each other a couple times and got to share some stories. I soon found out about the 114-mile trail called the Waitukubuli National Trail (WNT) on the island of Dominica in the Caribbean. The WNT takes you across dormant volcano rims, into lush rain forests, past graceful waterfalls, and through historical villages. What a stark contrast to the high alpine ridgeline we were perched upon at the moment. It sounded perfect for a future adventure.

I flew up the final bit of trail to Whitney. An amalgamation of freedom from the "pig" I had slogged on my back for 28 days and skills I've garnered from rock climbing made me hyper-prepared for this exact type of trail. Upon reaching the summit and letting out a victory whoop, I was quickly making new friends with Lisa and April, 60-year-old women who last summer completed the 165-mile Tahoe Rim Trail (TRT). They promptly offered me a sip of their Jack Daniels Honey Whiskey, and boy did it hit the spot. Their stories from the TRT left me wide-eyed and bushy-tailed

Looking south to the Whitney Range
from the tarn at Bighorn Plateau

just waiting to make my own adventure around Lake Tahoe. As I prepared my gear to descend, I found myself in conversation with fellow author Paul Barach, who recently published *Fighting Monks and Burning Mountains*, the story of his misadventures along the 750-mile Shikoku Pilgrimage Trail in Japan. Japan has always been on my mind as a country whose culture I must experience. There is no better way than to have a pilgrimage as a walking henro, visiting the eighty-eight Buddhist temples along the island—and if I have half as much of an adventure as Paul, I am in for a good time.

> IT STILL SEEMS TO ME ABOVE ALL OTHERS THE RANGE OF LIGHT, THE MOST DIVINELY BEAUTIFUL OF ALL THE MOUNTAIN-CHAINS I HAVE EVER SEEN.
>
> —*John Muir*

As I strolled down the summit of Whitney, knowing it literally was all downhill from here, I was able to reflect on the unforgettable sights, experiences, and people I got to meet along the trail. I was slightly dismayed by the fact that I never saw a bighorn sheep, all the sky pilots had passed their bloom, and lastly that I didn't get to see Seth and Hannah one last time, a father-daughter team I had met at MTR. Hannah, following family tradition by thru-hiking the JMT with dad on her 13th birthday, always had a smile on her face and little to complain about, except how bad she wanted warm, fluffy pancakes! Lo and behold, the next hikers coming up the summit were Seth and Hannah. Hugs and smiles were passed around as we caught up on the past two weeks of adventures. The trail would have felt incomplete if I didn't get to say goodbye to them. Shortly after, as I took one sharp switchback after another on the eastern side of Whitney, I ran right into a fully blooming sky pilot! I laughed to myself and looked around for a bighorn sheep—you never know . . . the Range of Light always provides.

OVERVIEW

As you descend beyond the two trail junctions to Kearsarge Pass, you emerge at Bubbs Creek with excellent views to the south of East and West Vidette Peaks and the Kearsarge Pinnacles to the east. There is another trail junction to the west following Bubbs Creek to Road's End in Kings Canyon National Park, a popular trailhead for the 42-mile Rae Lakes Loop. From here the trail meanders uphill past great campsites while following the gentle tumble of Bubbs Creek.

RESUPPLY LOCATIONS

Lone Pine Post Office
Phone: (760) 876-5681
Mail packages to:

(Your name)
c/o General Delivery
Lone Pine Post Office
121 East Bush St.
Lone Pine, CA 93545
Arriving by: ETA

Moonset and sunrise on the
Great Western Divide

Ascending out of the dense lodgepole pine forest, the trail leads up to the subalpine belt, passing many wildflowers like the vibrant purple rock fringe, and continues to the Kings-Kern Divide, which you will cross via the 13,155-foot Forester Pass, the highest on the trail yet. Views open up to 13,000-foot-high summits of University Peak, Junction Peak, and Mt. Stanford. Beneath the basin of the latter, you may be able to spot a V-shaped double waterfall in a patch of dark rock. There are excellent

Mount Whitney alpenglow
CLIFF LAPLANT (SIERRALARA.COM)

scenic campsites at 11,000 feet in the final stands of whitebark pines surrounded by one final alpine meadow; from here the camping is more sparse and exposed.

The final ascent of the pass takes you through a stark alpine terrain devoid of much plant life aside from the red mountain sorrel hiding under rocks in the shade. Weaving up switchbacks through the talus, you finally arrive at the summit of Forester Pass, discovered by Forest Service workers and becoming one of the final links to the JMT, which is also the official boundary to Kings Canyon National Park. Enjoy sweeping views of the terrain to the south, with Diamond Mesa flanking the east, 13,800-foot Caltech peak to your west, and the serrated skyline of the Kaweah group to the south.

EXCERPTS FROM THE BACKCOUNTRY

Keith Foskett (Fozzie) – PCT Thru-Hiker, Indie Author, and Blogger from the UK (keithfoskett.com)

On the summit of Mt. Whitney, there were around ten others up there, but the isolation was evident. We seemed miles from anywhere and felt, literally, like we were on top of the world. I'd seen photos, so I knew a little of what to expect, but the one part that amazed me was the distance the eye could see. It wasn't just the next ridge or mountain, it was ridges and mountains stretching away for distances I'd not experienced before.

Kristen Bor – Outdoor Enthusiast, Mountain Hardwear Ambassador (bearfoottheory.com)

My friend and I had spent the previous three weeks hiking through some of the country's most epic mountain scenery in California's Sierra Nevada. Alpine lakes, jagged peaks, roaring waterfalls, starry skies, and near perfect weather.

And now . . . it was almost over, and that was a tough pill to swallow. The next morning we would be watching the sunrise from the top of Mt. Whitney, the tallest peak in the lower forty-eight, and then a few hours later we would be back at my car. Pizza, ice-cold beers, a shower, and a comfy bed were at our fingertips, but mentally, I couldn't have been further away. I wasn't sure I was ready for the modern conveniences of daily life and to be reconnected to society. I felt like I could've stayed out there forever.

As I sat there watching the sun go down, thoughts about the future swirled through my head. A few months prior, I quit my job in Washington, DC, with plans to hike the John Muir Trail and start an outdoor-travel blog. Now that I had crossed the JMT off my list, I had to figure out what was next. But there at the spot, the answer seemed so obvious. I knew that the outdoors needed to be part of my daily life, not just an afterthought. So then and there, I made the commitment to myself that no matter what it took, I was going to make my new path work.

Mount Whitney at sunrise

Stop to marvel at the trail construction as you descend Forester Pass, completed in 1931. Switchbacks were blasted into the cliff and built up on stone barriers to descend the steep headwall. The trail weaves through open meadows, crossing many little streamlets dotted with wildflowers and dry sandy patches with a variety of buckwheat matting the ground. The trail reaches stands of foxtail pine, with nice camping options as you descend to the Tyndall Creek crossing, ranger station, and the junction with the Shepherd Pass Trail. Just beyond are the quaint Tyndall Frog Ponds, sporting an excellent camp area with food-storage lockers and a scenic pond where you are sure to run into some green Pacific chorus frogs.

The trail runs through a forest dominated by lodgepoles as you ascend to Bighorn Plateau, an otherworldly location that offers the first unobstructed views of Mt. Whitney. This Mars-like terrain has wide-open views in all directions and is a playground for many species of falcon like the kestrel. The trail descends past meadows bursting with Bigelow's sneezeweed as you approach two creek crossings that can be troublesome in the early season. At the second crossing, Wallace Creek, there is a trail

PHOTOGRAPHY TIP: PHOTOGRAPHING SUNSETS AND SUNRISES 📷

Most days in the Sierra Nevada will guarantee amazing light at sunrise and sunset, a.k.a. golden hour. Add some clouds and a body of water for the makings of an incredible photographic opportunity. Below are outlined some tips to help you prepare and photograph these fleeting moments in the mountains and help ensure success.

  You will want to arrive at your location at least 30 to 45 minutes before the sun hits the horizon for either sunset or sunrise, and remember, the sun doesn't have to be the subject of the image. Look at how the sunlight is affecting the surrounding landscape and determine your location based on that. At this point you will want to take some test shots to determine your exact angle and camera settings. Set your camera's f-stop somewhere between f8 and f16 to keep everything sharp. Adjust your shutter speed to compensate from here. If you have the opportunity to integrate a reflective body of water into the image, this will greatly increase the drama. Water will darken the reflection's exposure so you may need to use your tripod to balance out the light. Lastly, the weather plays a major role: If there are too many clouds, the sun may be blotted out. But if there is just the right amount, you will be in for a very colorful treat.

Sunset reflections over the Great Western Divide

Moonset behind the Whitney Range

Lone Pine Creek leads you back to
Whitney Portal

junction with the 63-mile-long High Sierra Trail (HST), which starts on the western slope in Sequoia National Park and finishes with the JMT at Mt. Whitney.

The trail ascends a lower ridge of Mt. Young through gentle terrain before it approaches the junction to the Pacific Crest Trail (PCT), which continues south to the border of Mexico, and a junction to Crabtree Meadows. From this point the trail turns due east into the lake basin west of Mt. Whitney, first going past a junction to the Crabtree Meadow ranger station where a large plastic bin contains WAG bags, required for human waste disposal in the Whitney zone. The JMT now follows Whitney Creek up past the last stands of lodgepoles and Timberline Lake, where camping is prohibited. Your eyes will quickly be drawn to the shoreline as it bursts with shooting stars and lupines during peak bloom season.

Your next major stop on the trail is the ultra-scenic Guitar Lake. Incomparable reflected views of the Kaweah range at sunset and sunrise, along with the imposing fluted faces of Mounts Whitney and Hitchcock, make this a high point for many hikers. Lots of camping can be found on the northern and eastern shores with little to no protection. This is also the last reliable source for water until the other side of Whitney. Here is where the steep switchbacks up the rocky monolith begin, weaving around large pinnacles, under granite overhangs, on and on to the trail junction at 13,500 feet, which then leads to the summit. Typically backpackers leave their pack here and take a daypack to the summit and back. Be sure to keep all your food and toiletries in your bear canister to protect them from small critters.

THE SNOW IS MELTING INTO MUSIC.
—*John Muir*

The final stretch of the official JMT takes you north up the ridgeline to Mt. Whitney, passing Mt. Muir, an excellent fifth-class rock scramble up the 14,000-foot summit. The rocky trail will give you little V-shaped slots with dizzying views down the eastern escarpment to Lone Pine, the first time you see this type of scenery on the trail. The trail turns back east and ascends the final plateau to the summit, signified by the emergency stone hut and large white plaque representing the end of the JMT and summit of Whitney. From here you can see many of the subranges traversed along the trail to the north and across the dry Owens Valley to the White Mountains in the east. Before you strike out on the final descent to Whitney Portal, find a nice spot to relax and soak in the Range of Light, mountains and valleys that have inspired so many people around the world to pursue their arts and physical passions.

GUITAR LAKE

There is no better way to say goodbye to the Sierra Nevada and the John Muir Trail than camping at Guitar Lake on one of your final nights here. This lake can be accessed a couple of ways and is worth the visit, with sweeping views across the lake off to the west of the Great Divide. And the Kaweah Range sunset and sunrise will never disappoint, especially if you are lucky enough to be here during a full moon. The terrain is very alpine (considering you are at 11,505 feet) and backs right up to the western slope of Mt. Whitney with the giant gabled Mt. Hitchcock to your south. You can expect temps to get quite cold here in the evenings and there is minimal protection from storms, so be aware of the weather before heading here.

Sources

Adams, Ansel. *Sierra Nevada: The John Muir Trail*. New York: Little, Brown and Company, 2006.

Adams, Ansel. *Yosemite and the Range of Light*. Boston: New York Graphic Society, 1979.

Asorson, Erik. *John Muir Trail Pocket Atlas*. 2nd ed. Yucca Valley, CA: Blackwoods Press, 2014.

Berger, Karen. *Hiking and Backpacking: A Complete Guide*. New York: W.W. Norton & Company, 1995.

Castle, Alan. *Trekking the John Muir Trail through the California Sierra Nevada*. 2nd ed. Milnthorpe, UK: Cicerone, 2015.

Farquhar, Francis P. *History of the Sierra Nevada*. Berkeley: University of California Press, 2007.

Fiddler, Claude. *The High Sierra: Wilderness of Light*. San Francisco: Chronicle Books, 1995.

Huber, N. King. "The Geologic Story of Yosemite National Park," US Geological Survey Bulletin 1595 (1987). https://pubs.usgs.gov/bul/1595/report.pdf.

Jones, Dewitt, and T. H. Watkins. *John Muir's America*. Portland, OR: Graphic Arts Center Publishing Company, 1976.

Kestenbaum, Ryel. *The Ultralight Backpacker: The Complete Guide to Simplicity and Comfort on the Trail*. Camden, ME: Ragged Mountain Press, 2001.

Konigsmark, Ted. *Geologic Trips: Sierra Nevada*. Mendocino, CA: GeoPress, 2007.

Laws, John Muir. *The Laws Field Guide to the Sierra Nevada*. Berkeley, CA: Heyday Books, 2007.

Little, Elbert L. *National Audubon Society Field Guide to North American Trees: Western Region*. New York: Alfred A. Knopf Inc., 1994.

Muir, John. *The Mountains of California*. New York: Modern Library, 2001.

Muir, John. *My First Summer in the Sierra*. New York: Mariner Books, 1998.

Muir, John, and Lee Stetson. *Wild Muir: Twenty-Two of John Muir's Greatest Adventures*. Yosemite National Park, CA: Yosemite Association, 1994.

Munz, Philip A. *California Mountain Wildflowers*. Berkeley: University of California Press, 1969.

Munz, Philip A., Diane Lake, and Phyllis M. Farber. *Introduction to California Mountain Wildflowers*. Berkeley: University of California Press, 2003.

National Park Service. *Geology at Devils Postpile National Monument* (2015). www.nps.gov/depo/learn/nature/geology.htm.

Pavlik, Robert C. *Norman Clyde: Legendary Mountaineer of California's Sierra Nevada*. Berkeley, CA: Heyday Books, 2008.

Resendes, Mary Ann. *Geology of the Sierra Nevada* (2012). www.sierrahistorical.org/geology-of-the-sierra-nevada/.

Roper, Steve. *Sierra High Route: Traversing Timberline Country*. Seattle, WA: The Mountaineers Books, 2014.

Secor, R. J. *The High Sierra: Peaks, Passes, Trails*. 3rd ed. Seattle, WA: The Mountaineers Books, 2009.

Stebbins, Robert C., and Samuel M. McGinnis. *Field Guide to Amphibians and Reptiles of California*. Revised edition. Berkeley: University of California Press, 2012.

Storer, Tracy I., Robert L. Usinger, and David Lukas. *Sierra Nevada Natural History*. Berkeley: University of California Press, 2004.

United States Geological Survey. *Geology and National Parks* (2005). https://geomaps.wr.usgs.gov/parks/province/pacifmt.html.

U.S. Forest Service. *Wilderness Hiking: Big Pine Canyon, Inyo National Forest*. www.fs.usda.gov/Internet/FSE_DOCUMENTS/stelprdb5195705.pdf.

Wenk, Elizabeth. *John Muir Trail: Data Book*. Birmingham, AL: Wilderness Press, 2014.

Wenk, Elizabeth. *John Muir Trail: The Essential Guide to Hiking America's Most Famous Trail*. 5th ed. Birmingham, AL: Wilderness Press, 2015.

Winnett, Thomas, and Kathy Morey. *Guide to the John Muir Trail*. 3rd ed. Berkeley, CA. Wilderness Press, 2001.

Winnett, Thomas, Jason Winnett, Kathy Morey, and Lyn Haber. *Sierra North: 100 Trips in California's Sierra*. Berkeley, CA. Wilderness Press, 2004.

Winnett, Thomas, Jason Winnett, Kathy Morey, and Lyn Haber. *Sierra South: 100 Trips in California's Sierra*. Berkeley, CA. Wilderness Press, 2004.

Top Ten Vistas & Side Trails

Vistas

CATHEDRAL LAKES

ISLAND PASS

GARNET LAKE

SHADOW LAKE

RAE LAKES BASIN

EVOLUTION BASIN

BEAR RIDGE

MUIR PASS

MATHER PASS

MT. WHITNEY

Side Trails

HALF DOME

CLOUDS REST

DONAHUE PEAK

MINARET LAKE

PAINTED LADY

TAWNY POINT

BENCH LAKE

CENTER BASIN

60 LAKES BASIN

WOTANS THRONE

Index

About the Author

Damon Corso, a freelance photographer, writer, and videographer, has been photographing and filming rock-climbing professionals since 2004 across the United States and Europe. His work can be found on the covers and in feature articles of a multitude of major magazines, including *Climbing, Rock & Ice, Deadpoint, Urban Climber, Los Angeles* magazine, *Time, National Geographic Adventure,* and *Exercise & Health.* His work is also on display at the Museum of Photography in Bad Ischl, Austria. Damon, his wife, Crystalyn, and their rescued chicken and pit bull currently live in Southern California, where he dreams of spending a majority of his time searching the High Sierra for untouched granite boulders.